54-250-99 $ 10.00 EC

v

Columbia University

Contributions to Education

Teachers College Series

No. 766

AMS PRESS
NEW YORK

MENTALLY SUPERIOR AND INFERIOR CHILDREN OF JUNIOR AND SENIOR HIGH SCHOOL AGE

A COMPARATIVE STUDY OF THEIR BACKGROUNDS, INTERESTS, AND AMBITIONS

By GLENN MYERS BLAIR

INSTRUCTOR IN EDUCATIONAL PSYCHOLOGY
UNIVERSITY OF ILLINOIS

SUBMITTED IN PARTIAL FULFILLMENT OF THE REQUIREMENTS FOR
THE DEGREE OF DOCTOR OF PHILOSOPHY IN THE FACULTY
OF PHILOSOPHY, COLUMBIA UNIVERSITY

Published with the Approval of
Professor Leta S. Hollingworth, Sponsor

BUREAU OF PUBLICATIONS
TEACHERS COLLEGE, COLUMBIA UNIVERSITY
NEW YORK
1938

Library of Congress Cataloging in Publication Data

Blair, Glenn Myers, 1908-
  Mentally superior and inferior children in the junior
and senior high school.

  Reprint of the 1938 ed., issued in series: Teachers
College, Columbia University. Contributions to educa-
tion, no. 766.
  Originally presented as the author's thesis, Columbia.
  Bibliography: p.
  1. Exceptional children--Education. 2. Everett,
Wash.--Public schools. I. Title. II. Series: Colum-
bia University. Teachers College. Contributions to
education, no. 766.
LC3969.B55 1972   155.9'2   71-176567

ISBN 0-404-55766-X

Reprinted by Special Arrangement with Teachers
College Press, New York, New York

From the edition of 1938, New York
First AMS edition published in 1972
Manufactured in the United States

AMS PRESS, INC.
NEW YORK, N. Y.   10003

TO
A. D.
AND
W. L. U.

ACKNOWLEDGMENTS

THE writer wishes to express his appreciation to the many individuals who assisted him in bringing the present study to completion. The following members of his research seminar gave many helpful suggestions which have been incorporated into the work: Dr. Rudolph Pintner, Dr. Harry Dexter Kitson, Dr. Percival M. Symonds, Dr. Mary T. Whitley, Dr. Robert C. Challman, Dr. Ruth Strang, and Dr. R. L. Thorndike. Much assistance in connection with the statistical phases of the study was given by Dr. Helen M. Walker and Dr. Warren G. Findley. At various stages of the investigation Dr. Arthur I. Gates and Dr. Ralph B. Spence also gave helpful criticism and advice.

Most of all, however, the author is indebted to Dr. Leta S. Hollingworth, his sponsor. Professor Hollingworth's wide acquaintance with the area under investigation and her stimulating counsel have been an invaluable source of assistance in developing the study.

Thanks are also due to Ruth V. Blair, the writer's wife, for her aid in performing much of the clerical work.

G. M. B.

CONTENTS

TABLES

xi

MENTALLY SUPERIOR AND INFERIOR CHILDREN IN THE JUNIOR AND SENIOR HIGH SCHOOL

CHAPTER I

INTRODUCTION

ALTHOUGH psychologists have been investigating the problem of individual and group differences since the time of Francis Galton,[1] there is still need for further research in this area. Within recent years our secondary schools have experienced an unprecedented growth. Evidence obtained from the United States Office of Education[2] discloses that there were more than twenty times as many children attending our high schools in 1934 as there were in 1890. Whereas formerly our secondary schools were made up of a somewhat selected group, this is certainly not the case today. Children of all levels of ability, with varying backgrounds, interests, and ambitions, are studying side by side.

Little or no provision is made in many of our secondary schools for anything like adequate guidance of these individuals.[3] In fact, educators are to a great extent ignorant of the types and magnitude of differences which exist in and between certain groups in their schools.

Although it is known that pupils of superior and inferior mental ability are to be found in every secondary school, little is known as to the extent and quality of other differences which separate these two groups.

The present study seeks to investigate this problem. There are a great many traits and characteristics in which an intellectually superior group and a retarded group might possibly differ. To study them all—or any great number of them—would be impossible in any one research project. The present investigation is lim-

---

[1] Francis Galton, *Hereditary Genius*. 1869.
[2] United States Office of Education Bulletin, 1935, No. 2, Chap. II of the *Biennial Survey of Education in the United States,* p. 9. Also see Bulletin, 1933, No. 2, Chap. I, p. 6.
[3] Franklin J. Keller and Morris S. Viteles, *Vocational Guidance Throughout the World: A Comparative Survey,* p. 37. 1937.

ited to a comparative study of the backgrounds, interests, and ambitions of mentally superior and inferior children enrolled in the junior and senior high school. These points were chosen for study because they have significance for the guidance of children of secondary school age.

Before outlining the present investigation in detail, a brief résumé of previous related studies will be made in the following paragraphs.

PREVIOUS STUDIES

The most notable research studies in the field of superior children have been carried on by Hollingworth[4] at Columbia, and Terman[5] at Stanford. These investigators have made a very thorough study of gifted children of elementary school age. Their technique, for the most part, has been to compare children who score in the highest centile of intelligence with an unselected group, and note differences that may exist. Among other things, Hollingworth[6] has found that gifted children are taller than average children, are stronger than average as measured by a dynamometer, possess greater speed on a tapping test, have fewer siblings than average, have brighter siblings than average, and possess greater facial beauty than do average children.[7] She found, however, that gifted children on the average do not possess greater musical sensitivity than unselected children,[8] nor are they able to broad jump or chin themselves better.[9]

Other research studies of gifted children at the elementary

---

[4] L. S. Hollingworth, *Gifted Children: Their Nature and Nurture*. 1926.
[5] L. M. Terman, *Mental and Physical Traits of a Thousand Gifted Children*. Genetic Studies of Genius, Vol. 1. 1925.
[6] L. S. Hollingworth, *op. cit.*
[7] L. S. Hollingworth, "Comparative Beauty of the Faces of Highly Intelligent Adolescents." *Journal of Genetic Psychology*, Vol. 47, Dec. 1935, pp. 268-281.
[8] L. S. Hollingworth, "Musical Sensitivity of Children Who Test Above 135 I. Q." *Journal of Educational Psychology*, Vol. 17, 1926, pp. 95-107.
[9] J. E. Monahan, and L. S. Hollingworth, "Neuromuscular Capacity of Children Who Test Above 135 I.Q." *Journal of Educational Psychology*, Vol. 18, 1927, pp. 88-96.

school level have been reported by Collmann,[10] Coy,[11] Jenkins,[12] McElwee,[13] and Witty.[14]

Almack and Almack[15] in 1921 studied fifty-one superior children in grades 7 to 12 at Eugene, Oregon. They concluded from their study that superior children were not queer, pathological, or erratic, and that as a rule the gifted pupils were more retarded according to their mental ages than any other group in the schools. They also studied the physical measurements, subject interests, and national origins of the superior group, but they utilized no control group in evaluating their findings.

Yates[16] published in 1922 a study which she made of twenty-five gifted high school seniors. She used as a control group twenty-five high school seniors of average mental ability. Her results showed little or no difference in the occupations of the fathers of the two groups, little or no difference in the education of the parents, and practically no difference in the health of the two groups. She reports that science was the most preferred subject of the superior group, and drawing the most preferred of the control group. It is, however, impossible to draw any general conclusions from this study because too few cases were investigated.

Deich and Jones[17] surveyed 316 high schools in Iowa in an effort to find the most superior senior in each. The representative student was selected by the superintendent or principal as the sole

[10] R. D. Collmann, *The Psychogalvanic Reactions of Exceptional and Normal School Children.* 1931.

[11] Genevieve Coy, *The Interests, Abilities, and Achievements of a Special Class for Gifted Children.* 1923.

[12] M. D. Jenkins, "Socio-psychological Study of Negro Children of Superior Intelligence." *Journal of Negro Education,* Vol. 5, 1936, pp. 175-190.

[13] E. W. McElwee, "A Comparison of the Personality Traits of 300 Accelerated, Normal, and Retarded Children." *Journal of Educational Research,* Vol. 26, 1932, pp. 31-34.

[14] Paul A. Witty, *A Study of One Hundred Gifted Children.* 1930.

[15] J. C. Almack and J. L. Almack, "Gifted Children in the High School." *School and Society,* Vol. 14, 1921, pp. 227-228.

[16] D. H. Yates, *A Study of Some High School Seniors of Superior Intelligence.* 1922.

[17] Charles Deich and Elmer E. Jones, *A Study of Distinguished High School Pupils in Iowa,* United States Office of Education Bulletin, No. 46. 1923.

judge. On the basis of questionnaires filled out by the superintendent or principal and by the pupil chosen, certain conclusions were reached. Girls were found to be predominant in the superior group as were also pupils from rural districts and from well-to-do families. The physical condition of the subjects was not below average; their modal age of graduation was 18; and 60 per cent intended to go to college. The study habits, scholarship, and mental ratings of these subjects were found to be superior. The method of selecting these individuals within the schools and the equalization of representation regardless of school size, however, cause one to doubt the reliability of the sampling obtained.

Terman[18] reported in 1925 the results of an investigation he conducted, using as subjects 309 gifted high school students. He studied a variety of characteristics possessed by these individuals. This research, however, was inconclusive, as Terman himself admits, because no control group was employed, and the data were gathered by many different schools with but little immediate supervision.

In 1930 Burks, Jensen, and Terman[19] made a follow-up study of the subjects investigated in 1925. Again no control group was used with which to compare the significance of their findings with respect to an average or a dull group. Their interest was to note whether or not gifted children tested after an interval of several years would still possess essentially the same qualities and characteristics that they first exhibited.

Lamson[20] in 1930 studied a group of fifty-six young gifted senior high school pupils. The purpose of this work was to "give an assemblage of facts with which to supplant popular opinion concerning the advisability of gifted children entering high school several years younger than the generality of their classmates." [21]

[18] L. M. Terman, op. cit.
[19] B. S. Burks, D. W. Jensen, and L. M. Terman, The Promise of Youth, Follow-Up Studies of a Thousand Gifted Children. Genetic Studies of Genius, Vol. III. 1930.
[20] E. E. Lamson, A Study of Young Gifted Children in Senior High School. 1930.
[21] Ibid., p. 2.

Her findings indicate that gifted children do not suffer in any respect from entering high school at an early age.

A study somewhat similar to Lamson's was reported by Moore[22] in 1933. Among other things Moore was concerned with the question of whether young gifted children should be encouraged to graduate from high school at an age as young as two years below average. From the results of the investigation, she draws the following conclusion:

From this we conclude that so far as college achievement as measured by objective tests and college grades is concerned, it is desirable to encourage gifted students to enter college at an age as young as fifteen or sixteen years. There is no evidence of any loss since the young gifted hold their own with the older gifted, and there is obvious reason for believing that these young pupils have saved something like two years, and have probably avoided habits of indolence which they might have acquired if they had refrained from occupying themselves with studies which constituted a real challenge to their intelligence and industry.[23]

In addition to the studies already reviewed, which have had for their purpose a direct study of superior children, several statewide surveys have been made which have indirectly contributed some information regarding gifted children. One of the earliest of these was conducted by Book.[24] During May, 1919, he tested 6,188 Indiana high school seniors, using the Indiana University Intelligence Scale, Schedule D. He also obtained certain personal data concerning these seniors. Following are listed some of the conclusions he reached from his study:

1. Superior pupils come from all types of schools, communities, and sections of the state, and from practically all occupational and economic classes.

2. The high schools are ill adapted to the varied capacities, interests, and vocational needs of their pupils.

[22] Margaret W. Moore, *A Study of Young High School Graduates.* 1933.
[23] *Ibid.*, p. 66.
[24] W. F. Book, *The Intelligence of High School Seniors.* 1922.

3. The high schools make little effort to locate and provide for their superior students.

4. The brightest seniors do not come from the wealthier homes, but from homes of average economic status.

More recently, Gerberich[25] has reported the results of the Iowa state-wide survey. A part of this study is concerned with superior high school seniors. The summary of his results with respect to the gifted group is as follows:

The highest decile pupils on the survey were chosen as a gifted group for special analysis. These students are selected on intellectual and economic standards, are markedly younger than the average age of the survey seniors, and consist of a greater percentage of boys than girls. Their college attendance numbers 68 per cent of the total gifted group, while only 35 to 40 per cent of Iowa high school graduates attend college. These facts indicate that to a certain degree the superior abilities and aptitudes of these gifted pupils are being cultivated in institutions of higher learning. On the other hand, the present occupations of those gifted pupils not now in school are somewhat lower on the occupational scale than their vocational choices, and many of them are in positions in which their superior abilities will receive no opportunity for expression. Furthermore, many students of inferior ability are entering colleges and universities, usually to be eliminated by selective processes with consequent injury to the student and marked educational waste.[26]

A study of pupils of low mentality in high school has been made rather recently by Portenier.[27] She compared sixty-six dull pupils of the West High School, Denver, Colorado, with a control group of average children. The groups were compared on the basis of a standardized achievement test, curriculum in which they were enrolled, school marks, teacher's ratings of character, economic status, satisfaction with school life, home life, and self, and on several miscellaneous factors. Her results seem to indicate that the groups differ in the parts of the achievement test

[25] J. R. Gerberich, *A Personnel Study of 10,000 Iowa High Schol Seniors.* 1930.
[26] *Ibid.,* p. 102.
[27] Lillian G. Portenier, *Pupils of Low Mentality in High School.* 1933.

dealing with paragraph meaning, geography, and arithmetic computation. Differences were also noted between the two groups with respect to teacher's marks in the more academic subjects; the courses for which they were enrolled; teacher's ratings for intelligence, leadership, originality, and general quality of work; the estimated number of books read per year; the number who plan to attend college; the estimate of time spent in home study; the feeling that school work is too difficult; and the percentage of friends in school.

The two groups showed little or no difference in the scores on the dictation test; the rating on socio-economic status; teacher's marks in music, physical education, industrial arts, and citizenship; teacher's ratings for lack of conceit, popularity with schoolmates, self-control, industry, cooperativeness, perseverance, dependability, ambition, etc.

There are several factors, however, which tend to make the findings of this study somewhat unreliable. They are as follows: (1) the experimental group consisting of thirty boys and thirty-six girls was too small a group from which to draw any very definite conclusions; (2) little or no attempt was made to ascertain whether the obtained differences were statistically reliable or possibly due to chance; (3) the experimental group consisted of pupils in grades 9 to 12, but the control group consisted entirely of pupils in grade 9.

The studies that have been reviewed indicate that, although much good work has been done in the area of gifted and retarded children, this is still a pioneer field, and further and more refined research is needed. There is particularly a need for thoroughgoing studies at the secondary school level which would explore the extent and types of differences which exist between mentally superior and inferior pupils. These two groups of individuals are in every school, and it is very important that in administering a sound guidance program education take into account their particular traits.

PURPOSE OF THE PRESENT STUDY

The present investigation is a comparative study of intellectually superior and inferior secondary school pupils. The superior group consists of 446 subjects and the inferior group, of 455 subjects. The mentally superior pupils have intelligence quotients which place them in the highest 15 per cent of the total population tested, while the mentally inferior pupils have intelligence quotients which place them in the lowest 15 per cent of the total population tested.

The purpose of this study is to see if any significant differences are to be found in certain background factors, interests, and ambitions of these respective groups. The *background factors* studied are birthplaces of parents, education of parents, occupations of fathers, occupations of grandfathers, and size of families. The *interests* analyzed include subject preferences, participation in school activities, hobbies, reading interests, and interest in world affairs. The *ambitions* investigated are those relating to the pursuance of further education, and the choice of a life's occupation. The influence which certain of the background factors exert upon certain of the interests and ambitions of the subjects is also studied.

The study does not propose to account for, or explain the genesis of, certain differences which may be found to exist between the two groups studied. The purpose is to determine the extent and type of differences that do exist, and to point out their implications for educational practice.

CHAPTER II

SUBJECTS, DATA, AND METHOD OF THE STUDY

THIS investigation was carried on in Everett, Washington, a city with a population of about 40,000, located twenty-five miles north of Seattle. The subjects of the study are mentally superior and inferior pupils of the junior and senior high schools who were in attendance during the academic year 1936–37. In the school system there are two junior high schools and one senior high school. The junior high schools are attended by pupils in grades 7, 8, and 9, and have a combined enrollment of approximately 1,500. The senior high school is composed of pupils in grades 10, 11, and 12, and likewise has an enrollment of about 1,500.

The entire student bodies of the junior and senior high schools were first given intelligence tests. For the senior high school, the Otis S-A Test of Mental Ability, Higher Examination, Form A was used. In the junior high schools, the Otis S-A Test of Mental Ability, Intermediate Examination, Form A, and the Terman Group Test of Mental Ability, Form A were employed. Each intelligence test was scored twice to insure accuracy. The distributions of the I. Q.'s, means, and standard deviations of the groups taking these tests are given in Table I.

In this study pupils whose intelligence quotients are one standard deviation or more above their respective group averages are labeled "Superior," while those pupils whose I. Q.'s are one standard deviation or more below average are classified "Inferior."

Using this technique the following sized superior and inferior groups were obtained:

GROUP	SUPERIOR (No. of Cases)	INFERIOR (No. of Cases)
Senior High School.................	222	230
Junior High School.................	224	225

Of the 222 pupils in the senior high school superior group,

TABLE I

DISTRIBUTION OF I.Q.'S OF PUPILS TESTED

SENIOR HIGH SCHOOL GROUP		JUNIOR HIGH SCHOOL GROUP			
Otis S-A Test of Mental Ability, Higher Examination, Form A $N = 1463$		Otis S-A Test of Mental Ability, Intermediate Examination, Form A $N = 778$		Terman Group Test of Mental Ability, Examination, Form A $N = 622$	
I.Q.	No.	I.Q.	No.	I.Q.	No.
135–139	3	135–139	1	155–159	1
130–134	6	130–134	2	150–154	0
125–129	18	125–129	11	145–149	0
120–125	59	120–124	36	140–145	1
115–119	109	115–119	90	135–139	5
110–114	213	110–114	129	130–134	10
105–109	308	105–109	130	125–129	36
100–104	291	100–104	122	120–124	52
95–99	226	95–99	98	115–119	72
90–94	141	90–94	68	110–114	83
85–89	57	85–89	43	105–109	92
80–84	25	80–84	25	100–104	86
75–79	6	75–79	14	95–99	65
70–74	1	70–74	7	90–94	55
		65–69	2	85–89	30
				80–84	13
				75–79	14
				70–74	6
				65–69	0
				60–64	1
Mean I.Q.	104.15	103.84		106.38	
S.D.	9.60	11.49		13.39	
Mean + 1 S.D.	113.75	115.33		119.77	
Mean − 1 S.D.	94.55	92.35		92.99	

127 are boys and 95 are girls. Of the 230 senior high school pupils in the inferior group, 104 are boys and 126 are girls. In the junior high school superior group of 224 individuals, 120 are girls and 104 are boys, while in the junior high school inferior group 109 are girls and 116 are boys.

The differences in sex proportions are not statistically significant, as can be seen in Table II. In no case does the difference divided by the standard error of the difference equal 3.00.[1] This result is dissimilar to that found by Terman[2] in his study of 309 gifted high school pupils. Of these 309 gifted high school pupils, Terman found 200 to be boys and 109 to be girls. Terman's finding in this respect, however, may be somewhat unreliable because of his method of selecting his subjects. In his study, only pupils nominated by teachers were tested. It is possible that a sex preference entered into these nominations.

TABLE II

SEX PROPORTIONS IN THE MENTALLY SUPERIOR AND INFERIOR GROUPS

| | SUPERIOR | | | INFERIOR | | |
	Boys	Girls	$D/\sigma D_p$	Boys	Girls	$D/\sigma D_p$
Senior High School....	57.2%	42.8%	2.16	45.2%	54.8%	1.45
Junior High School....	46.4%	53.6%	1.09	51.6%	48.4%	.48

Following the administration of the intelligence tests, all subjects in the present investigation were required to fill out questionnaires (see Appendix) which sought information regarding their backgrounds, interests, and ambitions. The subjects were also given a test[3] of knowledge of world affairs—a test of 100 questions covering national and international news for the period of July, 1936 to January, 1937.

Throughout the study the senior and junior high school groups are, for the most part, treated separately. That is, the bright senior high school group is compared with the dull senior high school group, and the bright junior high school group is compared with the dull junior high school group.

In interpreting differences, the following statistical techniques are employed: (1) Chi-square,[4] (2) Analysis of Variance,[5] and

[1] H. E. Garrett, *Statistics in Psychology and Education*, pp. 226-229. 1937.
[2] L. M. Terman, *Mental and Physical Traits of a Thousand Gifted Children*. Genetic Studies of Genius, Vol. 1, p. 560. 1925.
[3] National Current Events Test, American Education Press. 1937.
[4] R. A. Fisher, *Statistical Methods for Research Workers*, pp. 81-119. 1936.
[5] G. W. Snedecor, *Calculation and Interpretation of Analysis of Variance and Covariance*. 1934.

(3) Difference Divided by Sigma of Difference.[6] For studying relationships the Pearson r,[7] and the Tetrachoric r[8] for widespread classes are employed. For rating occupations the Brussell-Barr Scale of Occupational Intelligence[9] is used (this scale is given in the Appendix).

In the chapters to follow, the backgrounds, interests, and ambitions of superior secondary pupils will be compared with those of mentally inferior secondary school pupils. As was previously stated, the superior group is made up of those pupils whose intelligence places them in the highest 15 per cent, approximately, while the inferior group is composed of those pupils whose intelligence quotients fall in the lowest 15 per cent, of the 2,863 pupils tested.

[6] H. E. Garrett, *op. cit.*, pp. 210-229.

[7] *Ibid.*, pp. 251-288.

[8] C. C. Peters and W. R. Van Voorhis, *Statistical Procedures and Their Mathematical Bases*, pp. 269-277. 1935.

[9] E. S. Brussell, *A Study of the Composition of Juries of the District Court*, Thesis, University of Minnesota Library, 1930. (The scale is described in Part II of this thesis.)

CHAPTER III

BACKGROUNDS

In this chapter an analysis will be made of the backgrounds of the superior and inferior groups. To quote Huxley, "No man can say where they [gifted individuals] will crop up; like their opposites, the fools and the knaves, they appear sometimes in the palace and sometimes in the hovel." [1] The purpose of this section of the investigation is to see if the gifted and the ungifted spring equally often from the same sources. The background factors to be studied are the birthplaces of the parents, occupations of fathers, occupations of grandfathers, education of parents, and size of families.

BIRTHPLACES OF PARENTS

Of the 901 superior and inferior children who are the subjects of this study, 70.03 per cent were born in the State of Washington, the state where this investigation was carried on. This is, however, decidedly not true of their parents. Only 11.73 per cent of the parents were born in Washington. The remainder came from all parts of the United States and from many foreign countries. Thus was provided an excellent opportunity for comparing the birthplaces of the parents of bright children with the birthplaces of parents whose children rate low in intelligence tests.

In Table III the United States is divided into five sections, North Atlantic states, South Atlantic states, South Central states, North Central states, and Western states. This classification of states is that used by Cattell[2] in his analysis of the sections of the United States contributing most individuals to *American Men of Science*.

[1] N. V. Scheidemann, *The Psychology of Exceptional Children*, p. 231. 1931.
[2] J. McKeen Cattell, "The Distribution of American Men of Science in 1932." *American Men of Science*, Fifth Edition, pp. 1265-1266. 1933.

TABLE III

BIRTHPLACES OF PARENTS

Place	SENIOR HIGH GROUP		JUNIOR HIGH GROUP		COMBINED GROUP		$D/\sigma D_p$
	Superior $N=412$	Inferior $N=404$	Superior $N=384$	Inferior $N=324$	Superior $N=796$	Inferior $N=728$	
North Atlantic States (Maine, New Hampshire, Vermont, Massachusetts, Rhode Island, Connecticut, New York, New Jersey, Pennsylvania)	7.3%*	3.7%	3.9%	3.1%	5.7%	3.4%	2.17
South Atlantic States (Florida, Georgia, So. Carolina, No. Carolina, W. Virginia, Virginia, Maryland, Delaware)	1.0	2.5	1.8	2.5	1.4	2.5	1.56
South Central States (Kentucky, Tennessee, Alabama, Mississippi, Louisiana, Texas, Oklahoma, Arkansas)	3.9	4.5	2.4	6.8	3.1	5.5	2.30
North Central States (Minnesota, Wisconsin, Michigan, Nebraska, Kansas, Indiana, Illinois, Iowa, Ohio, N. Dakota, S. Dakota, Missouri)	45.9	43.8	46.4	38.0	46.1	41.2	1.92
Western States..... (Washington, Oregon, California, Montana, Idaho, Utah, Colorado, Wyoming, Arizona, New Mexico, Nevada)	18.7	14.1	25.0	17.9	21.7	15.8	2.96
Foreign Countries...	23.3	31.4	20.6	31.8	22.0	31.6	4.24

χ^2 for the combined group $= 18.01$ $n = 5$ $P = .003$

* This means that 7.3% of the parents of the bright senior high school pupils were born in the North Atlantic States.

The data presented in Table III show very marked differences to exist between the birthplaces of parents of mentally superior children and the birthplaces of parents of mentally inferior children. For the senior high school group, it is seen that 7.3 per cent of the parents of bright children were born in the North Atlantic states, while only 3.7 per cent of the parents of the dull children were born there. In like manner, it is found that parents of superior senior high school pupils were more frequently born in the Western states and the North Central states than were parents of pupils in the dull group. Studying the senior high school group still further, it is noticed that parents of pupils in the dull group were born in greater numbers in the Southern states and foreign countries than were parents of gifted pupils.

When the data for the junior high school group are analyzed, it is apparent that not a single reversal in the above findings takes place. Section for section the patterns are identical for both the junior and senior high school groups.

The junior and senior high school groups were combined and the chi-square test[3] was applied to see if these observed differences are statistically significant or whether they are due to a chance selection. For the combined table of six categories (the geographical sections), chi-square was found to be 18.01, with P equal to .003.[4] This indicates that a statistically significant difference is present which is not attributable to chance. In problems involving chi-square a P of .02 or less may be taken as indicative of a significant deviation from expectancy. From the data presented in Table III, it is also possible to tell in which sections the differences are most marked. Whereas chi-square tells whether there is a statistical difference for the table as a whole, $D/\sigma D_p$[5] tells whether the difference obtained for any particular section of the table is in itself statistically reliable. It is usually customary to take a $D/\sigma D_p$ of 3 as indicative of complete reliability. A $D/\sigma D_p$ greater than 3

[3] R. A. Fisher, *Statistical Methods for Research Workers*, pp. 81-119.
[4] Karl Pearson, *Tables for Statisticians and Biometricians*, Part I, Third Edition, pp. 26-28. 1930.
[5] H. E. Garrett, *Statistics in Psychology and Education*, pp. 210-229.

is to be taken as indicating just so much added reliability. Using this as a criterion, it is apparent that the differences found for the Western states and foreign countries are statistically reliable taken by themselves. For the South Central states, $D/\sigma D_p$ equals 2.30, which means that there are 99 chances out of 100 that the obtained difference is a real one. Likewise, for the North Atlantic states the $D/\sigma D_p$ of 2.17 indicates that the chances are 98.5 out of 100 that a real difference also exists for this section of the country.

The fact that parents of intellectually superior children greatly outnumber parents of intellectually inferior children in the Western states is not surprising when the data obtained from the tests given in the army during the World War are taken into account.[6] On the army tests, out of all the states in the Union the men from Oregon ranked first, the men from Washington ranked second, and the men from California ranked third. Wyoming ranked fourth, Idaho was sixth, Utah was seventh, and the remainder of the Western states were among the top states.

The finding in the present study that parents born in the Southern states contribute more children to the dull group than one would expect by chance, also harmonizes with the army test data. Every one of the Southern states ranked low on the army intelligence test.

When the data in Table III are rearranged so that the parents from Northern and Western states are put in one category, and the parents born in the Southern states are put in a second category, the chi-square test again reveals a statistically significant difference. In this case chi-square is equal to 6.695 and P is less than .01. This gives further confirmation to the evidence already presented in this chapter that parents born in the Northern and Western states who now live in Everett, Washington contribute more children to the gifted group than they do to the dull group, while parents born in Southern states give a greater proportion of children to the dull group than to the gifted group.

[6] R. M. Yerkes (Editor), *Psychological Examining in the United States Army*. Memoirs of the National Academy of Sciences. 1921.

These findings corroborate and supplement the work of Visher.[7] Visher made an analysis of *American Men of Science* and *Who's Who in America* and found the Northern states to be far more productive of leaders than the Southern states. Visher attributes this to differences in the quality of the stock of these respective groups, and to social conditions.

Although the underlying causes probably cannot with certainty be established, the data of this study, nevertheless, show a real difference to exist between the birthplaces of parents of intellectually superior children and those of parents of mentally inferior children.

OCCUPATIONS OF FATHERS

Two questions relating to occupations of fathers were included in the questionnaire which the 901 subjects filled out. The first question was: "What is the present occupation of your father?" and the second one was: "What other occupations has your father followed?" The purpose of the second question was twofold. First, it provided information which made the total occupational picture of the father more complete; and second, it gave some indication of the general occupational status of the father even though he might be at the time unemployed.

In order to make an objective comparison of the occupations of fathers of mentally superior children and those of fathers of mentally inferior ones, some sort of objective occupational scale was needed. The Brussell-Barr Scale of Occupational Intelligence[8] was finally selected for this purpose. This scale was recently used by Donald G. Paterson in his University of Minnesota Employment Stabilization Research.[9]

The scale consists of 243 occupations which were classified by

[7] Stephen S. Visher, "The Comparative Rank of American States," *American Journal of Sociology,* Vol. 36, March, 1931, pp. 735-757.

[8] E. S. Brussell, *A Study of the Composition of Juries of the District Court.* 1930.

[9] Donald G. Paterson, *Research Studies in Individual Diagnosis,* Vol. 3, No. 4, University of Minnesota Employment Stabilization Research Institute, p. 10. 1934.

twenty leading industrial psychologists according to the following six categories:

1. High Professional and Executive Occupations
   (Requiring very superior intelligence)

2. Lower Professional and Executive Occupations
   (Requiring superior intelligence)

3. Technical, Clerical, and Supervisory Occupations
   (Requiring high average intelligence)

4. Skilled Tradesmen and Low Grade Clerical Workers
   (Requiring average intelligence)

5. Semi-skilled Occupations
   (Requiring low average or slightly below average intelligence)

6. Unskilled Occupations
   (Requiring inferior intelligence only)

In constructing the scale, each of the 243 occupations was rated
separately by each of the twenty industrial psychologists. The
median rating given an occupation determined its final position in
the scale. The Brussell-Barr Scale correlates with the original Barr
Scale to the extent of .95 ± .006 for 114 common occupations.
This Pearson correlation was obtained by using the sigma scores
of the Brussell-Barr Scale as the units of one variable and the
probable error scores of the Barr Scale as the units of the second
variable. For the six categories given above, the C between the
Brussell-Barr Scale and the Barr Scale was found to be .81. The
entire Brussell-Barr Scale is given in the Appendix of this study.
The chief value of such a scale as this in rating occupations is that
it unquestionably approximates the facts more closely than would
the judgments of any one individual.

In using the scale, an occupation may be rated according to the
category in which it falls or it may be given a sigma value if this
is desired by the one using the scale.

In rating the occupations of the fathers, additional evidence
from the other parts of the questionnaire was sometimes taken
into consideration. For example, if a man who had not had college

training was reported as an "engineer," he would be rated in category 4 rather than in category 1 where the various technical engineering professions are listed.

Table IV shows how the occupations of fathers of mentally superior children compare with the occupations followed by fathers whose children are in the mentally inferior group. It is evident

TABLE IV

OCCUPATIONS OF FATHERS

Occupational Classification	SENIOR HIGH GROUP		JUNIOR HIGH GROUP	
	Superior $N = 209$	Inferior $N = 210$	Superior $N = 217$	Inferior $N = 211$
High professional and executive occupations	22	3	8	2
Lower professional and business occupations	25	1	20	7
Technical, clerical, and supervisory occupations	56	38	57	36
Skilled tradesmen, and low grade clerical workers	54	75	79	65
Semi-skilled occupations	44	72	45	79
Unskilled occupations	8	21	8	22

χ^2 for Senior High Group = 28.05 $n = 5$ $P = .00004$
χ^2 for Junior High Group = 19.31 $n = 5$ $P = .002$

from a glance at the table that great differences exist. For the senior high school group, 47 fathers of superior children are found in the professions and big business occupations, while only 4 of the fathers of inferior children are found in these same occupations. Still considering the senior high school group, it is seen, on the other hand, that 93 fathers of inferior children are found in the unskilled and semi-skilled occupations as compared to 52 fathers of superior children. The same general pattern prevails for the junior high school group. The chi-square test was applied to the senior and junior high school groups separately to see if these differences are statistically reliable. In both cases statistical reliability is indicated. For the senior high school group, the chances are only

4 out of 100,000 that the obtained difference is due to sampling errors, while for the junior high school group, the chances are 2 out of 1000 that the obtained difference is not a real one. In both cases these chances are too small to be given any consideration.

The 22 fathers of superior senior high school pupils who rank in the high professional and executive occupations are engaged in the following lines of work: physicians and surgeons, 5; civil engineers, 7; bankers, 3; editor of large city paper, 1; judge, 1; chemist, 1; heads of large companies, 4. The 3 fathers who rank in the high professions and have children in the senior high school mentally inferior group are engaged in the following types of work: doctors, 2; chemist, 1.

The 8 fathers in the unskilled occupations who have children in the gifted senior high school group are classified as follows: common laborers, 2; longshoremen, 4; lumber workers, 2. The 21 fathers in unskilled occupations who have children in the mentally inferior senior high school group do the following types of work: car loader, 1; common laborers, 7; lumber workers, 7; longshoremen, 5; elevator tender, 1.

The 8 fathers in the high professional and executive occupations who have superior children in the junior high schools are distributed as follows: civil engineers, 2; technical engineers, 2; banker, 1; big business executives, 3. The 2 fathers in this class who have inferior junior high school children are: banker, 1; doctor, 1.

The 8 unskilled fathers of superior junior high school pupils are classified as lumber workers, 2; day laborers, 4; longshoremen, 2; while the 22 unskilled fathers of inferior junior high school children are listed as: garbage collector, 1; lumber workers, 5; day laborers, 6; longshoremen, 7; section hands, 3.

Although the data presented here show considerable overlapping between the occupations of fathers of gifted children and the occupations of fathers of ungifted children, the differences found between the two groups are striking and statistically significant.*

---

* Terman found the average occupational status of parents of gifted elementary school children to be above the average for the general population. (Genetic Studies of Genius, Vol. 1, p. 83.)

OCCUPATIONS OF GRANDFATHERS

The occupations of the grandfathers of the subjects of this study were also rated by the Brussell-Barr Scale to see if there are any significant differences between occupations followed by grandfathers of mentally superior children and those followed by grandfathers of mentally inferior children. The findings are summarized in Table V. Again it is seen that differences exist between the superior and the inferior groups. In both the junior and the senior high school groups the grandfathers of gifted children are more numerous in the three highest occupational levels than are grandfathers of ungifted children. For the three lowest occupational levels the reverse is true. Here the percentage of grandfathers of the ungifted exceeds the percentage of grandfathers of the gifted. The pattern of differences is identical for both the junior and the senior high school groups.

TABLE V

OCCUPATIONS OF GRANDFATHERS

Occupational Classification	SENIOR HIGH GROUP		JUNIOR HIGH GROUP	
	Superior $N = 315$	Inferior $N = 274$	Superior $N = 303$	Inferior $N = 228$
High professional and executive occupations..........................	6.0%	2.9%	4.3%	3.9%
Lower professional and business occupations........................	6.4	2.5	6.3	2.2
Technical, clerical, and supervisory occupations........................	25.1	12.8	16.5	11.0
Skilled tradesmen, and low grade clerical workers......................	46.0	58.4	53.1	58.3
Semi-skilled occupations.............	13.0	19.0	17.2	20.2
Unskilled occupations...............	3.5	4.4	2.6	4.4

χ^2 for Senior High School Group = 14.61 $n = 5$ $P = .01$
χ^2 for Junior High School Group = 6.09 $n = 5$ $P = .29$

For the senior high school group, the chi-square test shows the obtained difference to be statistically reliable. In the junior high school group, although the differences are all in the same direction as those in the senior high school group, they are not sufficiently large to indicate statistical reliability by themselves.

For the senior high school group, over twice as many grandfathers of gifted children are found in the professional occupations as are grandfathers of ungifted children. The ratio is approximately the same for the junior high school group.

EDUCATION OF PARENTS

Are parents of highly intelligent children better educated than parents of less intelligent children? The data summarized in Table VI indicate that this is decidedly the case. The figures for the

TABLE VI

EDUCATION OF PARENTS

Amount of Education	Senior High Group		Junior High Group	
	Superior $N = 426$	Inferior $N = 420$	Superior $N = 402$	Inferior $N = 390$
College graduates.................	14.8%	3.6%	10.0%	4.6%
Some college work.................	9.4	4.8	10.0	5.6
High school graduates.............	15.7	13.1	24.6	16.2
Some high school work............	15.5	17.6	20.4	16.4
8th grade graduates...............	30.3	36.4	27.9	28.5
Less than 8th grade...............	14.3	24.5	7.2	28.7

χ^2 for Senior High School Group $= 17.05$ $n = 1$ $P = .0002$
χ^2 for Junior High School Group $= 14.40$ $n = 1$ $P = .0009$

senior high school group show that there are more than four times as many college graduates among the parents of mentally superior children as there are among parents of the mentally inferior group. On the other hand, there are about twice as many parents of inferior children with less than an eighth grade education as there are parents of superior children. For the superior senior high school group it is seen that there are approximately the same number of parents with less than an eighth grade education as there are college graduates. However, for the inferior senior high school group there are approximately seven times as many parents with less than an eighth grade education as there are college graduates. The facts are very much the same for the junior high school group. For the junior high school group there are four times as many parents of inferior children with less than an eighth grade education as there are parents of superior children.

When the chi-square test was applied, using the two categories "high school graduation and up" and "less than high school graduation," a statistically significant difference was found to exist between the education of parents of the gifted and ungifted groups. This difference is highly significant for both the junior and senior high school groups. The P for the senior high school group is .0002, and the P for the junior high school group is .0009.

SIZE OF FAMILIES

Do children of superior intelligence have fewer brothers and sisters than children of inferior intelligence? For the subjects of the present study the answer is quite plain. The data presented in Table VII show that children of superior mental ability on the average come from smaller families than do children of inferior mental ability. Combining the data for the junior and senior high school groups, it is seen that 73 superior children are "only children" as compared to 39 inferior children. In like manner, 135 superior children have only one brother or sister as compared to 93 inferior children who have only one brother or sister.

When it comes to large families, the inferior groups surpass the superior groups. This trend is particularly marked for the junior high school group, where it is seen that the inferior group supplies 28 families in which there are seven or more children, while the superior group has only 8 families of seven or more children. The two largest families of all come from the inferior groups. In the senior high school inferior group, there is one family of twelve children, and in the junior high school inferior group there is one family of thirteen children.

The average number of children per family for the senior high school superior group is 3.17, while the average number for the senior high school inferior group is 3.64. The difference divided

TABLE VII

SIZE OF FAMILIES

Number of Children in Family	SENIOR HIGH GROUP		JUNIOR HIGH GROUP	
	Superior $N = 222$	Inferior $N = 225$	Superior $N = 223$	Inferior $N = 221$
1	33	22	40	17
2	67	54	68	39
3	52	46	44	59
4	26	37	30	36
5	20	31	21	23
6	8	18	12	19
7	7	8	4	9
8	3	3	2	9
9	4	3	1	6
10	2	2	1	3
11	0	0	0	0
12	0	1	0	0
13	0	0	0	1
Average number of children per family	3.17	3.64	3.00	3.97
$\dfrac{\text{Difference}}{\sigma \text{ Difference}} =$		2.60		5.11

by the sigma of the difference equals 2.60, which indicates that the chances are 99.5 out of 100 that a true difference exists. For the junior high school group the difference in the size of families of the two groups is still greater. Here the average number of children per family for superior children is 3.00, and the average number per family for inferior children is 3.97. The difference divided by the sigma of the difference is 5.11. This is indicative of very marked statistical reliability.

CHAPTER IV

INTERESTS

ARE the interests of mentally superior secondary school pupils significantly different from those of mentally inferior secondary school pupils? This is an important question, since modern educational theory holds that pupil interest should be one of the criteria for determining educational practice.

In this chapter a comparative study is made of the subject preferences, school activities, hobbies, reading interests, and interest in world affairs of the mentally superior and inferior groups.

SUBJECT PREFERENCES

One of the items on the questionnaire reads: "Of all the subjects you have taken, name the one you like best." This information was desired in order to compare the mentally superior and inferior groups with respect to their most preferred subject. The data for the senior high school group are presented in Table VIII. By far the most liked subject of the superior boys is mathematics. Nearly 32 per cent of them state that it is the best subject they have ever taken. Only 8.0 per cent of the inferior senior high school boys give mathematics as their most preferred subject. The subject most liked by the mentally inferior boys is shop, 36 per cent of them listing it as their preferred subject. The superior senior high school girls like English best of all. Over 20 per cent of them give it as their most preferred subject. Home economics is the most popular subject of the mentally inferior senior high school girls, 29 per cent of them listing it as the best subject they have ever taken.

Other differences in the subject preferences may be noted in Table VIII. Superior boys tend to like science better than mentally inferior boys do. On the other hand, boys in the inferior group list history and the social sciences as their most preferred

25

subjects far more frequently than do the mentally superior boys. Mentally superior senior high school girls give mathematics and foreign languages as their most liked subjects in rather large numbers, while the mentally inferior girls list them scarcely at all.

A number of these differences between the subject preferences of the superior and inferior group are statistically significant. The greater preference of superior boys for mathematics as compared to inferior boys possesses marked statistical reliability. The difference in per cent divided by the sigma of difference is 5.41. The greater preference of mentally inferior boys for shop as compared to mentally superior boys is likewise statistically significant. The difference divided by the sigma of difference is 3.02. The greater liking of inferior girls for home economics as compared to superior girls also possesses statistical reliability, the difference in per cent divided by the sigma of difference being 3.57. Several others of these differences between the gifted and ungifted groups are very close to being statistically reliable, as can be inferred from the "$D/\sigma D_p$" columns of Table VIII.

TABLE VIII

SUBJECTS MOST PREFERRED BY MENTALLY SUPERIOR AND
MENTALLY INFERIOR SENIOR HIGH SCHOOL PUPILS

Subject	Boys			Girls		
	Superior $N = 126$	Inferior $N = 100$	$D/\sigma D_p$	Superior $N = 94$	Inferior $N = 124$	$D/\sigma D_p$
Mathematics.......	31.8%	8.0%	5.41	11.7%	3.2%	2.32
Science...........	19.8	13.0	1.39	6.4	6.4	.00
Shop.............	18.2	36.0	3.02			
Home economics...				10.6	29.0	3.57
History and social sciences	7.9	20.0	2.58	11.7	16.9	1.11
Commercial subjects	7.1	6.0	.33	14.9	16.9	.55
Music and art......	6.4	5.0	.45	9.6	11.3	.41
English...........	4.8	9.0	1.24	20.2	11.3	1.98
Foreign languages..	4.0	3.0	.42	14.9	4.8	2.46

The data presented in Table VIII give a very clear picture of the differences between the superior and inferior senior high school pupils with respect to their most preferred subjects. They do not, however, take directly into account the dislikes of the pupils for these subjects. It would be possible for a subject to be at the same time the most liked and also the most disliked for a given group. Perhaps a better method of determining the attitude of a group toward a subject would be to compute the ratio of those liking it to those not liking it. Since each pupil was also asked to give the subject he liked least, it has been possible to compute these ratios. These data are given in Table IX.

TABLE IX

SUBJECTS MOST LIKED AND LEAST LIKED BY MENTALLY SUPERIOR AND MENTALLY INFERIOR SENIOR HIGH SCHOOL PUPILS

	SUPERIOR			INFERIOR		
	Most Liked	Least Liked	Ratio	Most Liked	Least Liked	Ratio
			BOYS			
Mathematics..............	40	18	2.22	8	22	.36
Science...................	25	12	2.08	13	9	1.44
Shop.....................	23	0		36	6	6.00
History and social science....	10	33	.33	20	26	.77
Commercial subjects........	9	0		6	4	1.50
Music and art.............	8	1	8.00	5	0	
English...................	6	34	.18	9	30	.30
Foreign languages..........	5	24	.21	3	2	1.50
			GIRLS			
English...................	19	9	2.11	14	19	.74
Foreign language...........	14	9	1.56	6	7	.86
Commercial subjects........	14	2	7.00	21	4	5.25
History and social science....	11	37	.30	21	53	.40
Mathematics..............	11	23	.48	4	23	.23
Home economics...........	10	6	1.67	36	2	18.00
Music and art.............	9	6		14	1	14.00
Science..................	6	5	1.20	8	11	.73

A ratio of 1.00 indicates that a subject is liked and disliked by an equal number of individuals. A ratio of more than 1.00 means that more pupils of the given group like it than dislike it. Similarly, a ratio of less than 1.00 indicates that more pupils of the group dislike the subject than like it. By comparing the ratios of two different groups for the same subject, it is possible to obtain a measure of their respective attitudes toward that subject.

Referring to Table IX it is seen that judged by this criterion mathematics is still much more preferred by mentally superior senior high school boys than by those boys who score low on the intelligence tests. Although mathematics is given as the most preferred subject by very few inferior boys, it is given as the least liked subject by a great many. Over twice as many superior boys like mathematics as dislike it, while about three times as many inferior boys dislike mathematics as like it. Using this method, it is apparent also that English and foreign languages are still better liked by superior girls than by inferior girls. The difference between the interest of superior and inferior girls in home economics which was brought out in Table VIII is also strikingly brought out by this method.

Other interesting facts are brought out in Table IX. Although commercial subjects and shop are not the most preferred subjects of the superior boys, there is none of their group who gives them as being disliked. Music and art are also subjects that are seldom disliked by anybody.

The data summarized for the senior high school group, and presented in Tables VIII and IX, show on the whole that there are marked differences between the mentally superior and inferior groups with respect to certain subjects of the high school curriculum.

For the junior high school group included in this study, differences are not so marked between the preferred subjects of the superior and inferior pupils. For the most part, however, the differences follow the same general pattern as those for the senior high school group.* Mathematics is the preferred subject of 29.8 per cent of the superior junior high school boys, but is preferred

---

* In his study of elementary school children, Terman found, with certain exceptions, that gifted children are more interested than unselected children in school subjects which are abstract, and less interested in the "practical" subjects. (Genetic Studies of Genius, Vol. 1, p. 382.)

by only 18.1 per cent of the inferior junior high school boys. The difference in per cent divided by the sigma of difference is 2.05. Mathematics is also the best liked subject of 31.7 per cent of the superior junior high school girls, but it is preferred by only 22.9 per cent of the inferior junior high school girls. The difference divided by the sigma of difference is 1.52. Home economics is preferred by 20.2 per cent of the inferior junior high school girls, but by only 8.3 per cent of the superior junior high school girls. This difference divided by the sigma of the difference equals 2.59 and comes very close to being statistically reliable. It indicates that the chances are 99.5 out of 100 that mentally inferior junior high school girls prefer home economics to a greater extent than do mentally superior junior high school girls. The differences in other school subjects are small and do not approach statistical significance.

The fact that subjects are much more highly specialized in the senior high school probably accounts for greater differences in subject preferences being found between superior and inferior pupils at this level than at the junior high school level.

SCHOOL ACTIVITIES

The questionnaire used in this study included the following question: "In what school activities have you participated?" An analysis of the answers to this question shows, in the first place, that a greater per cent of superior pupils than inferior pupils at both the junior and senior high school levels take part in school activities. For the senior high school group, 66.2 per cent of the superior pupils report taking part in activities, while only 50.4 per cent of the inferior group report activities in which they have participated. The difference in these two percentages is statistically significant—$D/\sigma D_p$ equals 3.43. For the junior high school group, 66.5 per cent of the superior group report school activities, but only 48.9 per cent of the inferior group do so. The difference between these two percentages is again statistically reliable—$D/\sigma D_p$ equals 4.29.

Furthermore, the superior pupils who take part in school activities engage in more activities per person than do inferior pupils who likewise take part in school activities. Superior senior high school pupils taking part in activities list 2.1 activities per person, while inferior senior high school pupils taking part in school activities give on the average 1.6 activities per person. Similarly, superior junior high school pupils listing activities give on the average 1.8 activities per person, while members of the inferior group engaging in activities report only 1.3 activities per person.

Marked qualitative differences also exist between the superior and inferior groups with respect to the activities in which they participate. These differences are presented in tabular form in Table X. Forty-two members of the superior senior high school group have been elected to the Torch Society because of their high scholarship, but not a single member of the mentally inferior group has grades sufficiently high to qualify for membership. The superior senior high school group contributes seven members to the debate squad, but the group which stands in the lowest 15 per cent of intelligence contributes none. The superior groups of the senior and junior high schools provide large numbers of school officers and leaders, while the inferior groups contribute practically none. It may be somewhat surprising to note that three members of the inferior senior high school group are included among the school leaders. These three individuals have intelligence quotients which are among the highest of those in the inferior group. The offices they hold are "president of sophs," class officer, and business manager of the school paper. While the inferior groups of the junior and senior high schools contribute a total of three individuals to the two categories entitled "School Officers and Leaders" and "Staff Members of School Publications," the superior groups contribute seventy-three individuals to these same two categories.

In only one school activity are inferior pupils more numerous than superior pupils. That activity is athletics. This holds for both the junior and senior high school groups. This numerical superiority of the inferior groups over the superior groups in athletics is all the more surprising when it is remembered that the inferior groups do not engage in activities to as great an extent as do the superior groups. Sports and athletics comprise 37.5 per cent of all the activities mentioned by the senior high school inferior group, while they comprise only 17.1 per cent of the activities mentioned by the senior high school superior pupils. The great emphasis given to athletics by the inferior pupils is still more strikingly shown by the junior high school group. At this level, sports and athletics make up 63.7 per cent of all activities reported by the inferior group, while they make up only 23.3 per cent of the activities of the superior group.

TABLE X

SCHOOL ACTIVITIES OF MENTALLY SUPERIOR AND INFERIOR JUNIOR AND
SENIOR HIGH SCHOOL PUPILS

Activity	SENIOR HIGH GROUP		JUNIOR HIGH GROUP	
	Superior	Inferior	Superior	Inferior
Torch Society (national scholastic honorary society)	42	0		
Members of debate team	7	0		
School officers and leaders (editors, class officers, student body officers, etc.)	32	3	12	0
Staff members of school publications (not included above)	19	0	10	0
Sports and athletics	53	71	61	86
Musical organizations	40	35	83	28
Dramatics and theatricals	33	26	28	11
Clubs, committees, etc.	84	57	60	10

χ^2 for Senior High School Group = 56.23 $n = 7$ $P = .000000$
χ^2 for Junior High School Group = 53.67 $n = 5$ $P = .000000$

The chi-square test was applied to the data reported in Table X to see whether or not the table taken as a whole indicates a statistically reliable difference between the superior and inferior groups with respect to participation in school activities. Chi-square for the eight categories of the senior high school table was found to be 56.23, with P being .000000. Chi-square for the six categories of the junior high school data of the table was found to be 53.67, with a P also of .000000. These figures indicate that a very high degree of statistical reliability is present.

The only categories not showing marked differences are the two in the senior high school group labeled "Musical Organizations" and "Dramatics and Theatricals." In these two activities the superior senior high school pupils numerically exceed the inferior pupils very little.

HOBBIES

Two questions were included in the questionnaire relative to hobbies. They were: (1) "Do you have any hobbies?" and (2) "What are they?" Space was provided for listing the hobbies.

Analysis of the data collected for the 901 pupils of this study shows that superior pupils more frequently have hobbies than do mentally inferior pupils. This situation was found to exist for both the junior and senior high school groups. Whereas 11.3 per cent of the superior senior high school pupils report no hobbies, 24.8 per cent of the inferior senior high school pupils give none. This difference is statistically reliable, since $D/\sigma D_p$ equals 3.86. In like manner, 22.3 per cent of the superior junior high school students give no hobbies, as compared to 38.7 per cent of the inferior junior high school who report none. This difference is also statistically significant, as $D\sigma/D_p$ is 3.81.

In addition to quantitative differences, qualitative differences were found to exist between the hobbies enjoyed by superior children and inferior children. In Table XI are presented several hobbies where this difference is apparent. Combining the data for junior and senior high school groups, it is seen that forty-seven superior pupils give reading as one of their hobbies, while only eleven pupils in the inferior groups do so. Fifty-one superior junior and senior high school pupils give as one of their hobbies the building of various sorts of models, whereas only sixteen members of the inferior group give this form of activity as a hobby. Fourteen pupils of superior mentality give photography as a hobby, as compared to one inferior pupil who does so. Likewise fourteen superior pupils list writing as a hobby, while none of the inferior pupils list it as such. Superior pupils also list as hobbies fishing, hunting, boating, hiking, skiing, and camping much more frequently than do inferior pupils. This is interesting when it is remembered that inferior pupils take part in school athletics more frequently than do superior pupils. The explanation may be that superior pupils, while not caring so much for competitive school athletics, take an interest in these more non-competitive forms of athletics, and develop them as hobbies. Another possible explanation might be that because mentally superior pupils come on the average from the higher economic levels, greater opportunity of engaging in such sports as boating, skiing, etc., is provided them.

TABLE XI

HOBBIES OF MENTALLY SUPERIOR AND INFERIOR JUNIOR AND SENIOR
HIGH SCHOOL PUPILS

Hobby	SENIOR HIGH GROUP		JUNIOR HIGH GROUP	
	Superior	Inferior	Superior	Inferior
Reading	25	10	22	1
Building models (airplanes, boats, etc.)	29	11	22	5
Photography	11	1	3	0
Writing (poetry, etc.)	8	0	6	0
Outdoor sports (fishing, hunting, boating, hiking, skiing, camping)	48	21	13	5
Sewing, knitting, cooking	5	12	6	9
Collecting	102	114	111	85

χ^2 for Senior High School Group $= 22.41$ $n = 6$ $P = .001$
χ^2 for Junior High School Group $= 21.34$ $n = 6$ $P = .001$

Sewing, knitting, and cooking are listed as hobbies by inferior pupils at both the junior and senior high school levels more frequently than by mentally superior pupils. There is also one other hobby in which the inferior group either equals or excels the superior group—that is in making collections. At the senior high school level the number of inferior pupils reporting various collecting activities numerically exceeds that of superior pupils. Furthermore, collecting activities comprise 43.2 per cent of all the hobbies reported by inferior senior high school pupils, while collecting activities make up only 28.1 per cent of the hobbies reported by the superior group. For the junior high school group, collecting activities form 43.6 per cent of all hobbies listed by the inferior group, but make up only 41.7 per cent of hobbies given by the superior group.

Many hobbies other than those given in Table XI were reported by both superior and inferior pupils. As there were so few of any one type, it was impossible to use them in making comparisons between the groups being studied.

The chi-square test was applied to the seven categories of Table XI. For both the junior and senior high school groups the pattern of differences proved to be statistically significant. Chi-square for the senior high school group was 22.41, with P being .001. Chi-square for the junior high school group was 21.34, with P also being approximately .001.

READING INTERESTS

The subjects of this investigation were asked to "Name two books you have enjoyed reading," and "Name two magazines you enjoy reading."

The book listed most frequently by the superior senior high school boys was *Mutiny on the Bounty,* and the one given most frequently by the inferior senior high school boys was *Oregon Trail.* The superior senior high school girls listed *Gone with the Wind* more than any other book, while the prime favorite of the mentally inferior senior high school girls was *Little Women.*

The junior high school superior boys listed *Tom Sawyer* more often than any other book, while the mentally inferior boys gave *Silver Chief* the greatest number of listings. By far the most popular book of both the mentally superior and inferior junior high school girls was *Little Women.*

At both the junior and senior high school levels the superior boys listed more books on biography, history, science, and travel than did the mentally inferior boys. Over 21 per cent of all books listed by mentally superior senior high school boys were on biography, history, science, or travel, but only 12 per cent of the books given by the mentally inferior senior high school boys were of this nature. This difference divided by the standard error of the dif-

TABLE XII

MAGAZINES READ BY MENTALLY SUPERIOR AND INFERIOR
SENIOR HIGH SCHOOL PUPILS

Type of Magazine	BOYS		GIRLS		TOTAL		$D/\sigma D_p$
	Superior $N=243$	Inferior $N=182$	Superior $N=183$	Inferior $N=230$	Superior $N=426$	Inferior $N=412$	
Scientific............ (Popular Mechanics, Popular Science, Short Wave and Television, National Geographic, Modern Mechanics, Scientific American, Modern Science, etc.)	15.2%	15.4%	2.7%	1.3%	9.9%	7.5%	1.20
Wild West, Detective, Mystery, Movie, and Pulp Magazines............ (Western Story, Wild West Weekly, True Detective, Detective, Shadow, Astounding Stories, Movie Screen, Movie Mirror, Hollywood, Pep Stories, etc.)	7.0	19.2	3.8	10.0	5.6	14.1	4.17
Sport................ (Field and Stream, Yachting, Outdoor Life, Hunting and Fishing, Sports Afield, etc.)	5.8	5.5	.0	.0	3.3	2.4	.82
Magazines for Boys and Girls .... (American Boy, American Girl, Boy's Life, Open Road for Boys, Boys World, etc.)	13.6	10.4	2.2	2.2	9.9	5.8	2.16
General Magazines (not included in above classifications) Five - and Ten - cent Magazines.......... (Liberty, Colliers, McCalls, Saturday Evening Post, Ladies Home Journal, Womans Home Companion, etc.)	23.0	31.9	30.1	44.8	26.1	39.1	4.06
Fifteen-cent Magazines and Up............ (Reader's Digest, American Magazine, Harpers, Esquire, Fortune, Coronet, Forum, Good Housekeeping, Nation, Cosmopolitan, Scribners, etc.)	33.3	17.6	61.2	41.7	45.3	31.1	4.18

ference equals 2.43. While this ratio does not quite reach statistical certainty, it nevertheless indicates that the chances are 99.3 out of 100 that a true difference exists. Of all the books enjoyed by the superior junior high school boys, 14.7 per cent were on biography, history, science, or travel, whereas only 9.7 per cent of

TABLE XIII

MAGAZINES READ BY MENTALLY SUPERIOR AND INFERIOR
JUNIOR HIGH SCHOOL PUPILS

Type of Magazine	Boys		Girls		Total		$D/\sigma D_p$
	Superior $N=193$	Inferior $N=163$	Superior $N=218$	Inferior $N=140$	Superior $N=411$	Inferior $N=303$	
Scientific..............	20.2%	14.7%	5.0%	1.4%	12.2%	8.6%	1.57
Wild West, Detective, Mystery, Movie, and Pulp Magazines	17.6	20.9	4.6	20.7	10.7	20.8	3.61
Sport.................	3.6	4.3	.0	.0	1.7	2.3	.55
Magazines for Boys and Girls	35.2	35.6	22.9	18.6	28.7	27.7	.29
General Magazines (Not included in above classifications) Five- and Ten-cent Magazines...........	14.5	17.8	33.9	40.0	24.8	28.1	1.00
Fifteen-cent Magazines and Up.............	8.8	6.7	33.5	19.3	21.9	12.5	3.36

the choices of the inferior boys were of this type. The difference divided by the sigma of the difference is 1.56. Practically no difference was found at either the junior or senior high school levels between the interests of superior and inferior girls in this type of reading.

More significant differences were found between the reading interests of superior and inferior pupils when the magazines they enjoyed were analyzed. The data for the senior high school group are presented in Table XII, while the data for the junior high school group are summarized in Table XIII.

It is seen in Table XII that mentally inferior senior high school pupils list wild west, detective, mystery, movie, and pulp magazines far more frequently than do mentally superior pupils. This is true for both boys and girls. The difference is statistically reliable, as the difference between the two percentages divided by the standard error of the difference equals 4.17. The same is true for the junior high school group, as can be seen in Table XIII. Whereas 20.8 per cent of all the magazines given by the mentally inferior junior high school group are of the wild west, detective, mystery, movie, and pulp variety, only 10.7 per cent of the magazines given by the superior group are of this type. This difference is also statistically significant.

For scientific magazines, sport magazines, and magazines for boys and girls, the differences are too small to be statistically reliable.

Marked differences are noted, however, between mentally superior and inferior children when the prices of the magazines they read are taken into consideration. All magazines not falling under one of the first four classifications of Table XII or Table XIII were classified according to price. At both the junior and senior high school levels, the superior pupils read far more expensive magazines than do mentally inferior pupils. Over 45 per cent of all the magazines listed by the superior senior high school pupils are found in that group where the price is fifteen cents and up, while only 31 per cent of the magazines enjoyed by the inferior senior high school group fall in that class. This difference is statistically significant. For the junior high school group the difference in this respect is also statistically reliable. General magazines costing five and ten cents are, on the other hand, more frequently read by pupils in the intellectually inferior group. Marked statistical reliability is obtained for the senior high school group.

Although the magazines costing fifteen cents and up are on the whole somewhat more scholarly and difficult to read than those costing less, the greater incidence of superior pupils reading them can probably be traced to an economic factor. In an earlier chapter it was found that the mentally superior pupils on the average come from higher economic levels than do the mentally inferior pupils. For this reason the higher priced magazines are probably more available to them than to the mentally inferior pupils.

The data of this study also reveal that pupils in the ungifted groups do not indicate reading interests so frequently as the mentally superior pupils. This is particularly true with respect to magazines. Sixty-one mentally inferior junior high school pupils do not report enjoying any magazines. Only ten superior junior high school pupils fail to list any magazines. In the senior high school thirteen inferior pupils give no magazines, as compared to six for the superior group. Considerable numbers of the inferior pupils are able to report only one magazine that they enjoy reading. The data show that forty-seven mentally inferior junior and senior high school pupils give just one magazine, while twenty-three superior junior and senior high school pupils list only one.

These data suggest that children in the lower intelligence levels read much less than do pupils of superior intelligence. The data presented in the section on hobbies also lend support to this conclusion. There it was found that inferior pupils gave reading as a hobby far less frequently than did the mentally superior pupils.

INTEREST IN WORLD AFFAIRS

How do the secondary pupils who rate in the highest 15 per cent of intelligence compare with their fellow classmates who rate in the lowest 15 per cent when it comes to knowledge of what is going on in the world? In order to answer this question the superior and inferior pupils of this study were given the National Current Events Test of 1937. This is a test covering national and international news for the period of July, 1936 to January, 1937. The test contains one hundred questions and requires forty minutes for its administration. There are six parts to the test, as follows: (1) History in the News; (2) Important Names in the News; (3) Words in the News; (4) The U. S. Constitution in the News; (5) General Current Information; and (6) By Their Words Ye Shall Know Them.

Under part 1, such questions as the following were asked (the students were instructed to place an X before the word or words which most accurately completed the thought of each sentence) :

President Roosevelt, in 1936, received: —— (1) the first unanimous vote; —— (2) the largest number of electoral votes; —— (3) benefit of the greatest split vote in the history of our country.

A variety of such questions as this one covered national affairs. Foreign affairs under part I were covered by questions such as the following:

One of the bloodiest civil wars has been raging in —— (1) France; —— (2) Russia; —— (3) Spain.

The subject matter of the other five parts of the examination booklet was tested by means of the matching tests, completion tests, and multiple choice tests similar to the examples given above. Using the split-halves technique and the Spearman-Brown[1] "prophecy" formula, the writer found the reliability coefficient of this test to be .92 ± .036.

In Table XIV the distribution of the scores of the mentally superior and inferior groups is presented. It is evident that an extremely marked difference exists between bright and dull secondary school pupils with respect to their knowledge of what is happening in the world. The differences are equally pronounced at both the junior and senior high school levels. The superior senior high school pupils get on the average 78.84 out of the 100 questions correct, while the mentally inferior senior high school pupils get, on the average, only 52.29 correct. This difference divided by the standard error of the difference equals 20.27, which indicates that a most reliable difference is present between the two groups. The mentally superior junior high school pupils make an average score of 57.53, while the mentally inferior group, on the average, gets only 32.52 out of the 100 questions correct. The difference in this case divided by the standard error of the difference is 18.00. This again points to a marked statistically reliable difference.

A very striking bit of evidence of the relationship of intelligence

[1] William Brown, *The Essentials of Mental Measurement*, p. 102. 1911.

TABLE XIV

DISTRIBUTION OF SCORES OF MENTALLY SUPERIOR AND INFERIOR
PUPILS ON THE NATIONAL CURRENT EVENTS TEST

Number of Correct Answers	SENIOR HIGH GROUP		JUNIOR HIGH GROUP	
	Superior $N = 206$	Inferior $N = 206$	Superior $N = 191$	Inferior $N = 190$
96–100	5	0	0	0
91–95	15	2	1	0
86–90	38	2	3	0
81–85	43	8	11	0
76–80	30	6	10	0
71–75	26	5	17	0
66–70	24	16	19	1
61–65	11	18	18	4
56–60	9	24	26	6
51–55	3	13	12	3
46–50	2	25	25	10
41–45	0	32	18	12
36–40	0	23	17	23
31–35	0	16	8	33
26–30	0	11	3	46
21–25	0	0	2	26
16–20	0	0	1	16
11–15	0	1	0	9
6–10	0	0	0	1
Average Score	78.84	52.29	57.53	32.52
$\dfrac{\text{Difference}}{\sigma \text{ Difference}} =$		20.27		18.00

to knowledge of world affairs is the fact that the gifted junior high school pupils make a higher average score on the test than do the ungifted senior high school pupils. Their scores are respectively 57.53 and 52.29. Although the inferior senior high school pupils are on the average three years farther along in school, and three or more years older than the superior junior high school pupils, they nevertheless know less of events that are taking place in the world.

It might be objected that the reason mentally superior children know more about world affairs than do mentally inferior children is that they come on the average from better homes where they may more frequently hear their parents discuss such affairs. In order to test whether or not this might be the case, the author employed a technique[2] for holding the occupations of the fathers of gifted and ungifted groups constant while studying the differences in their scores on the current events test. The groups studied were the mentally superior sophomore boys and mentally inferior sophomore boys. The number of cases in each group were respectively 38 and 45. Using the Johnson and Neyman technique and continuing the analysis by means of Snedecor's [3] table, an F of 77.1 was obtained. This indicates that a highly significant difference in knowledge of world affairs still exists between the mentally superior and inferior groups, even when the occupations of the fathers are held constant.

A further idea of the close relationship that exists between knowledge of world affairs and intelligence can be gathered from the fact that the writer obtained for 370 sophomores a Pearson r of .58 ± .02 between scores of the Otis S-A Test of Mental Ability and the world affairs test used in this study.

[2] Palmer O. Johnson and Jerzy Neyman, "Tests of Certain Linear Hypotheses and Their Application to Some Educational Problems," *Statistical Research Memoirs*, Vol. 1, pp. 57-93, June, 1936.
Stanislaw Kolozziejczyk, "On an Important Class of Statistical Hypotheses," *Biometrika*, Vol. 27, pp. 161-190, March, 1935.
[3] G. W. Snedecor, *Calculation and Interpretation of Analysis of Variance and Covariance*, pp. 88-91. 1934.

CHAPTER V

AMBITIONS

"In this country, where men and women of ability have arisen and continue to rise from the lowest economic and social levels to positions of leadership in all fields of activity, one should expect youth to set out for the highest educational and vocational goals. A problem is presented for guidance workers, however, to help students judge their ability accurately and to plan programs in harmony with it." [1]

To what extent do secondary school pupils of superior and inferior ability make educational and vocational choices commensurate with their abilities? In this chapter a study is made of the ambitions of mentally superior and inferior pupils of junior and senior high school rank, to see what differences exist, and to determine the magnitude of these differences. Certain background factors which were presented in a previous chapter will be related to the ambitions of the respective groups.

EDUCATIONAL AMBITIONS

Junior high school group. One would probably expect that a considerable number of pupils who are in the lowest 15 per cent of their group with respect to intelligence would plan to finish their schooling at the end of the ninth grade. This is, however, not the case, as can be readily seen from the evidence in Table XV. These data indicate a practically universal tendency for children of all degrees of mental ability to plan for a high school education. Of the pupils in the mentally superior group 97.8 per cent plan to go to high school, while in the inferior group, 93.3 per cent have definite intentions of continuing their education beyond the junior high school.

[1] Leonard V. Koos and Grayson N. Kefauver, *Guidance in Secondary Schools,* p. 446. 1934.

TABLE XV

PLANS OF MENTALLY SUPERIOR AND INFERIOR JUNIOR HIGH SCHOOL
PUPILS WITH RESPECT TO ENTERING SENIOR HIGH SCHOOL

	Superior Group $N = 224$	Inferior Group $N = 225$
Number planning to go to senior high...........	219	210
Number planning to drop school at the end of the junior high school course....................	3	12
Number who are not sure what they will do......	2	3

TABLE XVI

COURSES MENTALLY SUPERIOR AND INFERIOR JUNIOR HIGH SCHOOL
PUPILS PLAN TO TAKE IN SENIOR HIGH SCHOOL

Course	BOYS Superior $N=103$	Inferior $N=107$	GIRLS Superior $N=116$	Inferior $N=104$	TOTAL Superior $N=219$	Inferior $N=211$	$D/\sigma D_p$
College preparatory .	35.9%	15.9%	30.2%	7.7%	32.9%	11.8%	5.41
General course......	2.9	7.5	3.5	9.6	3.2	8.5	2.30
Commercial........	9.7	6.5	31.9	38.5	21.5	22.3	.20
Vocational shops....	17.5	21.5			8.1	10.9	1.00
Home economics....			3.4	2.9	1.8	1.4	.37
Don't know........	27.2	42.1	24.1	35.6	25.6	38.9	3.02
Miscellaneous courses	6.8	6.5	6.9	5.7	6.9	6.7	

There are, however, twelve members of the inferior group as compared to three for the superior group who have definite intentions of dropping school at the end of the junior high school course. These twelve inferior pupils give as their projected plans the following: 1—"Join the C.C.C. camp"; 1—"Get a job delivering groceries"; 1—"Take up fishing"; 1—"Work in a theater"; 1—"Become an accordian player"; 1—"Are to become a mecanice"; 1—"Find work"; 5—"Don't know." Of the three pupils of superior mental ability who do not contemplate going to high school, two state that they don't know what they will do, and one states that he will get a job. These replies show quite clearly that those dropping school at the end of the ninth grade do not have visions of entering occupations of very high standing. The plans of those in the inferior group are somewhat in line with their abilities, but the plans of the three from the superior group are very much out of line.

The pupils who indicated their intention of entering senior high school were asked to state the courses they planned to pursue in the senior high school. The data relative to this question are summarized in Table XVI.

The superior junior high school pupils plan to take the college preparatory course more frequently than do the members of the mentally inferior group. The difference is statistically significant.

Mentally inferior pupils, on the other hand, plan to take the general course in greater numbers than do superior pupils. The difference, though rather marked, does not quite reach statistical certainty.

Little or no difference is found between the superior and inferior groups with respect to their plans to take the commercial, vocational, or home economics courses. In no case is the difference found to be statistically significant.

Intellectually superior junior high school pupils are, however, more certain of what courses they will take in the senior high school than are the members of the intellectually inferior group. Whereas 38.9 per cent of the inferior pupils state they do not know what course they will take in high school, only 25.6 per cent of the superior ones do not know the type of course they propose to take. The difference between these two percentages is statistically significant. The superior and inferior groups are both to quite a large extent uninformed as to what courses are offered in the senior high school. This fact is clearly shown by the rather large number of pupils who plan to take courses not offered there. Eleven members of the superior group plan to take such courses. They are as follows: archeology, architectural engineering, medical courses, electrical engineering, engineering, school teaching, and nurses' course. Likewise eleven members of the inferior group plan to take courses in high school which are not offered. The courses are: engineering, nurses' course, seamanship, arithmetic, and forestry.

The subjects were also asked whether or not they planned eventually to enter college or university. The data presented in Table XVII show that 56.7 per cent of the intellectually superior group state definitely that they plan to go to college, while 37.3 per cent of the pupils in the lowest 15 per cent of intelligence also state that they plan to go to college. The difference between these two percentages is statistically significant. This means that there is a true tendency for the brighter pupils to plan to go to college in greater numbers than less gifted pupils.

TABLE XVII

PLANS OF MENTALLY SUPERIOR AND INFERIOR JUNIOR HIGH SCHOOL PUPILS WITH RESPECT TO GOING TO COLLEGE

	BOYS		GIRLS		TOTAL		
	Superior $N=104$	Inferior $N=116$	Superior $N=120$	Inferior $N=109$	Superior $N=224$	Inferior $N=225$	$D/\sigma D_p$
Definitely planning to go to college...	59.6%	37.9%	54.2%	36.7%	56.7%	37.3%	4.22
Not planning to go to college..........	40.4%	62.1%	45.8%	63.3%	43.3%	62.7%	4.22

Although brighter pupils plan to go to college in greater numbers than mentally inferior pupils, the fact nevertheless remains that 37.3 per cent of pupils standing in the lowest 15 per cent of intelligence also plan for a college or university career.

A recently devised formula makes it possible to compute a correlation coefficient between two variables when only the tails of the distributions are employed.[2] Using this technique, a tetrachoric r of .16 with a $P.E.$ of .025 was obtained between intelligence and the tendency to plan for a college education. This correlation coefficient, although significantly positive, is nevertheless very low. It indicates that at the junior high school level, intelligence plays

[2] C. C. Peters and W. R. Van Voorhis, *Statistical Procedures and Their Mathematical Bases*, pp. 269-277. 1935.

a very minor role in influencing pupils' choices in the matter of planning for a college education. With a more thorough and scientific guidance program in effect, this extremely low correlation between intelligence and tendency to plan for a college education could probably be raised considerably.

Senior high school group. Each member of the bright and dull senior high school groups was asked to state whether or not he planned to finish high school. The results are arranged in Table XVIII.

TABLE XVIII

PLANS OF MENTALLY SUPERIOR AND INFERIOR SENIOR HIGH SCHOOL
PUPILS WITH RESPECT TO FINISHING SENIOR HIGH SCHOOL

	Superior Group $N = 222$	Inferior Group $N = 230$
Planning to finish senior high school.............	99.6%	96.1%
Planning to drop school before finishing..........	.0	3.9
Not sure.......................................	.4	.0

It is evident that practically every child in both the superior and inferior groups plans to finish his high school course. No member of the superior group in intelligence says that he does not plan to finish high school. Among the group which stands in the lowest fifteen per cent in intelligence only nine indicate they plan to drop school before the completion of their course. Time has certainly changed things. In an early investigation in New York City, Van Denburg[3] discovered that 53 per cent of the high school students considered high school education as unessential or of doubtful value, and 48 per cent of these same students were without definite intentions to finish the high school course.

Of the nine mentally inferior individuals who plan to drop school before finishing, six are girls and three are boys. The plans of the girls are as follows: "Take up beauty work"; "Get a job as an usher in a theater"; "Get married"; "No one's business but

[3] Joseph K. Van Denburg, *Causes of the Elimination of Students in Public Secondary Schools in New York City,* p. 69. 1911.

mine"; "To work"; and "I am going to stay at home." The three
boys plan the following careers: "Get on a boat or join the navy";
"Work in a mill"; and "Work in a shop where mechanics are
used." Pupils today seem to be aware that a high school education
is necessary if they are to get ahead in the world. These nine individuals who plan to drop high school do not picture for themselves any lofty careers.

As with the junior high school group, the senior high school
subjects were asked if they expected to enter college or university
when they finished high school.

TABLE XIX

PLANS OF MENTALLY SUPERIOR AND INFERIOR SENIOR HIGH SCHOOL
PUPILS WITH RESPECT TO ENTERING COLLEGE OR UNIVERSITY

| | Boys | | Girls | | Total | | |
	Superior $N=127$	Inferior $N=104$	Superior $N=95$	Inferior $N=126$	Superior $N=222$	Inferior $N=230$	$D/\sigma D_p$
Definitely planning to go to college...	64.6%	26.9%	53.7%	19.8%	59.9%	23.0%	8.58
Not planning to go to college..........	24.4	57.7	37.9	65.9	30.2	62.2	7.27
Doubtful and "don't know"..........	11.0	15.4	8.4	14.3	9.9	14.8	1.58

As can be seen from Table XIX, greater proportions of mentally superior pupils plan to go to college than of mentally inferior pupils. The percentages are respectively, 59.9 per cent and 23.0
per cent. This again is a statistically reliable difference. Although
the difference between the superior and inferior groups is a reliable one, the correlation between intelligence and tendency to plan
for a college education is far from being high. The tetrachoric r^4
for the senior high school group was found to be .31 with a $P.E.$
of .024. This correlation is considerably higher than that which
was found for the junior high school group (.16). Senior high
school pupils seem to be more aware of what is required at col-

[4] C. C. Peters, and W. R. Van Voorhis, op. cit., pp. 269-277.

lege and what ability is necessary to meet these requirements than are junior high school pupils. This fact is also brought out in Table XX, where it is seen that as mentally inferior pupils progress to higher grade levels a smaller percentage of them plan to enter college.

TABLE XX

PERCENTAGE OF MENTALLY SUPERIOR AND INFERIOR PUPILS AT EACH
SUCCESSIVE GRADE LEVEL PLANNING FOR A COLLEGE EDUCATION

Grade	Superior Group	Inferior Group
7th	51.4%	44.1%
8th	57.8	32.8
9th	61.9	32.3
10th	60.0	24.1
11th	59.0	22.6
12th	60.4	21.4

A correlation of .31, however, cannot by any stretch of the imagination be considered a high correlation. If it is held that a university education should be open only to those who can profit from the type of training there provided, a much higher correlation should exist. This correlation could, no doubt, be raised by providing a program of scientific guidance in the schools which would encourage those with exceptional mental ability to plan for a college education, and encourage those with very limited mental equipment to plan for a type of activity commensurate with their ability. There are, in fact, studies[5] which show that this can be done. In the Hedge and Hutson study,[6] the educational plans of 201 juniors and seniors in high school were recorded in September. Guidance was given these subjects, and in May their choices were again recorded. The results of the study show that whereas the average I. Q. of pupils planning to go to college was 108.1 in September, in May the average I. Q. of pupils planning

[5] J. W. Hedge and Percival W. Hutson, "A Technique for Evaluating Guidance Activities," *School Review,* Vol. 39, 1931, pp. 508-519.
[6] *Ibid.*

for a higher education was 111.4. This study also shows that whereas eleven pupils in the lowest quarter in intelligence planned to go to college in September, only one planned to do so in May.

There are, however, certain factors operating which are hard to overcome, and which make the task of guidance workers, who would seek to raise the correlation between intelligence and plans for higher education, quite difficult. Parents who themselves have good educations and who come for the most part from the higher economic levels often want their children to have the best educations possible regardless of the mental ability of their offspring. On the other hand, parents who have had limited opportunities for an education and who may belong to the lower economic levels of society may not see the necessity of educating a bright child or may be financially unable to do so. Data from the present investigation show that certain of these background factors operate to reduce the correlation between intelligence and tendency to plan for a college education. In Table XXI it is clearly seen that when the intelligence of the children is held constant, the education of the parents plays a role in determining which children shall plan to go to college.

TABLE XXI

RELATION OF EDUCATION OF PARENTS TO EDUCATIONAL AMBITIONS OF
MENTALLY SUPERIOR AND INFERIOR SENIOR HIGH SCHOOL PUPILS

	SUPERIOR GROUP		INFERIOR GROUP	
Education of Parents	Planning for College $N = 256$	Not Planning for College $N = 169$	Planning for College $N = 96$	Not Planning for College $N = 327$
College graduates..........	19.9%*	6.5%	7.3%	2.4%
Some college work..........	12.5	5.3	9.4	3.7
High school graduates.......	18.8	10.7	17.7	11.9
Some high school work......	17.2	13.6	17.7	17.7
Eighth grade graduates......	21.1	43.7	30.2	38.2
Less than eighth grade.......	10.5	20.1	17.7	26.0
	$\chi^2 = 18.67 \quad n = 5$		$\chi^2 = 11.64 \quad n = 5$	
	$P = .0019$		$P = .035$	

* This means that 19.9% of the parents of superior children planning to go to college are themselves college graduates.

For the intellectually superior group of children, 19.9 per cent of the parents of those children planning to go to college are themselves college graduates, while only 6.5 per cent of the parents of those children not planning to go to college are college graduates. The trend is consistent all the way down the table. Parents of mentally superior children planning for a higher education are better educated than are parents of mentally superior children not planning to enter schools of higher learning. The difference is statistically reliable.

The same general tendency is noted when the data for the mentally inferior group are examined. Whereas 7.3 per cent of the parents of mentally inferior children planning to go to college are college graduates, only 2.4 per cent of the parents of mentally inferior children not going to college are college graduates. In like manner throughout the rest of the table it is seen that dull children whose parents are well educated plan to go to college in much greater numbers than do dull children whose parents are not well educated.

TABLE XXII

RELATION OF OCCUPATIONAL CLASSIFICATION OF FATHERS TO
EDUCATIONAL AMBITIONS OF MENTALLY SUPERIOR AND
INFERIOR SENIOR HIGH SCHOOL PUPILS

Occupational Classification of Fathers	Superior Group		Inferior Group	
	Planning for College $N = 130$	Not Planning for College $N = 79$	Planning for College $N = 48$	Not Planning for College $N = 162$
Professional, executive, and big business..............	30.0%*	10.1%	6.3%	.6%
Technical, clerical, supervisory, and skilled tradesmen..	56.2%	46.8%	58.3%	52.5%
Semi-skilled and unskilled occupations................	13.8%	43.0%	35.4%	46.9%
	$\chi^2 = 10.00$ $n = 2$ $P = .007$		$\chi^2 = 5.91$ $n = 2$ $P = .05$	

* This signifies that 30.0% of the fathers of superior children planning to go to college are classified in the professional, executive, and big business occupations.

In Table XXII, the fact is also illustrated that when intelligence is held constant, the economic status of the home is also an important factor in determining which children shall go to college. Thirty per cent of the fathers of superior children planning to go to college or university belong to the professional, executive, and big business classes, while only 10.1 per cent of the fathers of mentally superior children not planning to go to college belong in these occupational categories. Only 13.8 per cent of the fathers of bright children who have high educational ambitions come from the semi-skilled and unskilled occupations, but 43.0 per cent of the fathers of bright children not planning for a higher education come from these lowly occupations. The difference between the occupations of fathers of superior children planning to go to college and the occupations of fathers of superior children not planning to do so is statistically significant. The same general pattern holds for the mentally inferior group. Fathers of mentally inferior children who plan to enter college or university come more frequently from the higher occupational levels than do fathers of mentally inferior children not expecting to pursue a higher education.

These facts suggest the possibility that the excessively high ambitions of less able pupils are often originated or stimulated by parents. The data also suggest that many brilliant children do not develop ambitions commensurate with their abilities because they are held back by the environment from which they come.

A well-planned guidance program in the schools can do much to lessen the harmful effects of these disturbing background factors. When parents support excessively high ambitions in a child, guidance workers should confer with them much in the same manner as they would with the child, and sympathetically interpret to them the evidence on his capacities and interests, pointing out to them the requirements for success in the projected program, and the chances of the child's meeting these requirements. The school should not permit the educational interest of a pupil to be jeopardized by mistaken conceptions of his parents without first giving them the basis for making more accurate judgments concerning the child. In dealing with very bright children who come from homes where there is little stimulation to strive for higher goals, and where there is often small or no financial backing, the guidance program can also be of service. In the first place, the pupil can be given the needed encouragement, and in the second place, a program may possibly be worked out whereby he will be able to finance his education in an institution of higher learning.

Each pupil who stated that he planned to enter college or university was asked what course he intended to pursue there. The courses proposed by the intellectually superior and inferior pupils are given in Table XXIII. Engineering is the most popular subject of both the bright and dull groups. Although superior pupils plan to take engineering in somewhat greater numbers than do inferior pupils, the difference is too small to be statistically significant. The difference between the two percentages divided by the standard error of the difference is only 1.51. Besides engineering, superior pupils also tend to select teaching, journalism, pharmacy, and liberal arts somewhat more frequently than do pupils of low mentality. On the other hand, a larger percentage of pupils of inferior intelligence choose forestry, nursing, physical education, home economics, and vocational subjects than do the very bright pupils. Both groups select medicine, law, science, music, drama, and art to about the same extent. The outstanding point to be gathered from the data in Table XXIII is that the overlapping of the choices of the two groups is very great. Many pupils with I. Q.'s in the seventies and eighties plan university courses in engineering, teaching, medicine, law, etc. The chances of a pupil with an I. Q. of seventy or eighty succeeding in any of these courses are practically nil. These pupils are in senior high school. At this stage of their development such inappropriate plans take on a serious aspect. Such wide-spread maladaption indicates lack of guidance somewhere along the line. The school must accept at least part of the responsibility for this ineffective guidance of its pupils.

Since the data which have been presented in this section were collected, 128 of the mentally superior and inferior subjects of

TABLE XXIII

COURSES PLANNED FOR COLLEGE AND UNIVERSITY BY MENTALLY
SUPERIOR AND INFERIOR SENIOR HIGH SCHOOL PUPILS

Course	Mentally Superior Group $N = 133$	Mentally Inferior Group $N = 53$
Engineering	19.5%	11.3%
Teaching	9.0	5.7
Business	8.3	7.6
Journalism	7.5	.0
Medicine	6.8	5.7
Law	4.5	5.7
Science	4.5	5.7
Architecture	3.0	1.9
Nursing	3.0	5.7
Pharmacy	2.3	.0
Forestry	2.3	5.7
Physical education	2.3	5.7
Liberal arts	2.3	.0
Music	2.3	1.9
Drama	.8	1.9
Home economics	.8	7.6
Art	.8	.0
Foreign service	.8	.0
Criminology	.0	1.9
Psychology	.0	1.9
Vocational	.0	5.7
Naval	.0	1.9
"Don't know what course."	19.5	17.0

this study have graduated from high school. Of the members in the intellectually superior group, 24.7 per cent have already enrolled in some college or university, while 9.3 per cent of the mentally inferior pupils who have graduated have likewise enrolled in an institution of higher learning. It is interesting to compare these figures with the data given in Table XX. There it was seen that 60.4 per cent of the mentally superior high school seniors planned to go to college, and 21.4 per cent of the intellectually inferior high school seniors likewise planned for a college education. The per cents of each group who have already entered college do not as yet equal the per cents of each group who originally planned to do so. However, a considerable number from each group will still probably enter college or university. Some of these pupils were graduated in mid-year and are undoubtedly postponing registration until the fall term. Others may have decided to remain out of school for a year and work, before going on to the university.

VOCATIONAL AMBITIONS

The following question relating to vocational choice was included in the questionnaire: "What occupation do you expect to follow as a life's work?" In Table XXIV are listed the percentages of the respective groups who answered this specific question and gave their proposed plan for a life's career.

TABLE XXIV

PERCENTAGE OF MENTALLY SUPERIOR AND INFERIOR PUPILS STATING THE OCCUPATION THEY EXPECT TO FOLLOW AS A LIFE'S WORK

	BOYS		GIRLS	
	Superior	Inferior	Superior	Inferior
Senior High School..........	75.6%	72.1%	84.2%	63.5%
Junior High School..........	76.9%	69.8%	68.3%	61.5%

There are no statistically significant differences between the percentage of superior children and inferior children definitely stating their choice of life's occupation, except in the case of senior high school girls. Eighty-four per cent of the bright senior high school girls list careers—other than marriage—they expect to follow, as compared to approximately sixty-three per cent for the dull senior high school girls. The difference in the two percentages divided by the standard error of the difference equals 3.63, which indicates that a real difference is present which cannot be attributed to a chance selection. The other differences, though small and not statistically reliable, are all in the same direction, and suggest that mentally superior pupils more frequently have definite vocational plans than do mentally inferior pupils of junior and senior high school age.

Qualitative differences in the vocational choices of the mentally superior and inferior secondary pupils are clearly evident in the data presented in Table XXV. The Brussell-Barr Scale was the instrument used in classifying the vocational choices of the subjects.

Over sixty-three per cent of the mentally superior senior high school boys who listed their choices select occupations in the higher and lower professional groups as compared to 24 per cent for the mentally inferior boys. Likewise 45 per cent of superior junior high school boys select the professions and big business occupations as compared to 17.2 per cent of the junior high boys in the duller group. There is shown a consistent tendency straight through Table XXV for the junior and senior high school boys of superior mental ability to choose occupations on higher levels than those chosen by mentally inferior boys. This tendency is statistically significant for boys in both the junior and senior high school groups.

It is interesting to note that girls do not aspire to enter the professions in anything like the proportions that boys do. However, when the occupational choices of mentally superior senior high school girls are compared with those of the less intelligent senior high school girls, a statistically reliable difference is found. Whereas 28.8 per cent of superior senior high school girls listing choices plan to enter the professions and big business, only 3.8 per cent of the senior high school girls of low mental ability contemplate such careers. The differences in the vocational choices of bright and dull junior high school girls are not so marked, although they follow the same general pattern.

A further striking feature of the data presented in Table XXV is the large number of mentally inferior boys at both the junior and senior high school levels who aspire to enter the professions and executive occupations. These boys all rank approximately in the lowest fifteen per cent of the groups tested on the basis of intelligence. None of these inferior senior high school boys have an Otis Higher Examination I. Q. above 94, and none of the in-

TABLE XXV

TYPES OF OCCUPATIONS SELECTED AS LIFE CAREERS BY MENTALLY
SUPERIOR AND INFERIOR JUNIOR AND SENIOR HIGH SCHOOL PUPILS

Occupational Classification	SENIOR HIGH SCHOOL				JUNIOR HIGH SCHOOL			
	Boys		Girls		Boys		Girls	
	Superior $N = 96$	Inferior $N = 75$	Superior $N = 80$	Inferior $N = 80$	Superior $N = 80$	Inferior $N = 81$	Superior $N = 82$	Inferior $N = 67$
High professional and executive occupations...	49.0%	18.7%	3.8%	2.5%	40.0%	12.3%	7.3%	1.5%
Lower professional and business occupations.......	14.6	5.3	25.0	1.3	5.0	4.9	15.8	4.6
Technical, clerical, and supervisory occupations.........	21.9	28.0	63.8	72.5	33.8	19.8	72.0	70.1
Skilled tradesmen and low grade clerical workers	11.5	40.0	6.2	8.7	11.2	40.7	4.9	13.4
Semi-skilled occupations.....	3.1	5.3	1.2	15.0	8.7	17.3	.0	10.4
Unskilled occupations.......	.0	2.7	.0	.0	1.3	4.9	.0	.0
	$x^2 = 14.27$		$x^2 = 14.59$		$x^2 = 16.10$		$x^2 = 8.48$	
	$n = 5$		$n = 5$		$n = 5$		$n = 5$	
	$P = .014$		$P = .012$		$P = .006$		$P = .133$	

ferior junior high school boys have an Otis Intermediate Examination I. Q. above 92.

In order to get an objective estimate of the relationship that exists between intelligence and the tendency for boys to plan for careers which fall in the professions and executive positions, tetrachoric correlations were worked out. The boys were already classified as being superior and inferior, so in order to obtain a fourfold table it was necessary only to classify the boys as planning or not planning to enter the professions and executive occupations. The professions and executive occupations include those occupations which rate in the two highest occupational categories of Table XXV. The technique employed was the one devised by Peters and Van Voorhis.[7]

The tetrachoric correlation between intelligence and tendency for junior high school boys to plan to enter the higher occupational levels was found to be .27 ± .042. The tetrachoric r between intelligence and tendency of senior high school boys to plan to enter the professions and executive positions was found to be .35 ± .037.

Both of these correlations, though significantly positive, are very low. Since success in the higher occupational levels is very largely determined by intelligence, much higher correlations should be in existence. Pupils with I. Q.'s in the seventies, eighties, and nineties have little or no chance of success in any of the occupations which are listed in the two highest categories of the Brussell-Barr Scale.

The specific occupations selected by the subjects of both superior and inferior intelligence are given in the Appendix of this study. There it is seen that pupils in the mentally inferior groups plan to enter the following professions in the following numbers: engineers, 10; physicians and surgeons, 6; lawyers, 2; architects, 2; forestry specialists, 3; chemists, 3; psychiatrist, 1; high school teachers, 7; accountants, 1; journalists, 1; veterinarians, 1; grade school teachers, 11.

In making their choices for life occupations, pupils are undoubtedly influenced by certain home factors, such as the economic status of their parents. Such disturbing influences would tend to lower the correlation between intelligence and tendency for pupils to select occupations requiring a great deal of intelligence. For the senior high school group the relationship between occupations of the fathers and choice of occupations of the senior high school boys was studied, with intelligence of the boys being held constant. It was found that a statistically significant difference exists between the vocational choices of mentally superior boys whose fathers belong to the higher occupational levels and the vocational

[7] *Op. cit.*, pp. 269-277.

choices of mentally superior boys whose fathers engage in the lower occupational pursuits. The gifted boys whose fathers are engaged in the higher occupations tend to select occupations on a somewhat higher level than do the gifted boys whose fathers are employed in the more lowly occupations. Chi-square was found to be 43.28, twenty degrees of freedom being employed. This gave a P of less than .01. A similar tendency was also noted in the vocational choices of mentally inferior senior high school boys. The difference, however, did not reach statistical certainty. Chi-square was 24.76 for twenty degrees of freedom. This gave a P of .20.

As was pointed out in the section on educational ambitions, the school must take the responsibility of providing a program of guidance which will assist in raising the correlations between ambition and ability. Low correlations between ambition and ability indicate that education is failing to perform its major function, which should be to bring about the maximal adjustment of each individual to the realities of life. In cases where parents facilitate the maladjustment of the pupil by encouraging inappropriate ambitions, the guidance service of the school should extend to the parents. Most parents would welcome any scientific information the school could give them relative to the needs of their children, provided it is given in the proper manner.

CHAPTER VI

SUMMARY AND CONCLUSIONS

THE purpose of the present study was to see if any significant differences were to be found in certain background factors, interests, and ambitions of intellectually superior and inferior pupils of junior and senior high school age. The senior high school group consisted of 222 mentally superior pupils, and 230 mentally inferior pupils. The junior high school group was composed of 224 mentally superior pupils, and 225 mentally inferior ones. Approximately 3,000 junior and senior high school pupils were first tested. Those pupils whose I.Q.'s were one standard deviation or more above their respective group averages were classified as "Superior," and those pupils whose I.Q.'s fell one standard deviation or more below average were labeled "Inferior."

Throughout the study, comparisons have been made between the superior and inferior groups. The general findings of the study are summarized as follows.

1. When the birthplaces of parents of bright children were compared with the birthplaces of parents of children in the dull groups, statistically significant differences were found to exist. The patterns of differences were identical for both the junior and senior high school groups. Parents born in the North Atlantic states, the North Central states, and the Western states contribute more children to the mentally superior groups than to the inferior groups. On the other hand, parents born in the South Atlantic states, South Central states, and foreign countries contribute a much larger percentage of children to the mentally inferior groups than to the mentally superior groups.

2. When the occupations of the fathers of the subjects of this study were rated by the Brussell-Barr Scale, statistically significant differences were found to exist between the occupations followed by fathers of gifted subjects and the occupations followed

59

by fathers of the ungifted subjects. Fathers of the gifted children come much more frequently from the higher occupational classifications than do fathers of the mentally inferior pupils. Using the Chi-square technique, the differences were found to be highly reliable at both the junior and senior high school levels. Whereas seventy-five fathers of gifted children were found to follow professional and executive occupations, only thirteen fathers of the ungifted children were found in these occupations.

3. The occupations of the grandfathers of mentally superior pupils were also found to rate higher on the Brussell-Barr Scale than the occupations of the grandfathers of mentally inferior pupils. This tendency was found to exist for both the junior and senior high school groups. For the senior high school group, the chi-square test showed the obtained difference to be statistically reliable. In the junior high school group, although the differences were all in the same direction as those in the senior high school group, the magnitude of these differences was not sufficient to indicate statistical reliability.

4. Parents of gifted junior and senior high school pupils were found to be much better educated than parents of the ungifted pupils. The obtained differences were found to possess high statistical reliability for both the junior and senior high school groups. Whereas 103 parents of gifted children were found to be college graduates, only thirty-three parents of the ungifted were found to have that much education.

5. Mentally superior pupils have fewer brothers and sisters than do mentally inferior pupils. The difference was found to be marked for both the junior and senior high school groups. The difference divided by the standard error of the difference for the senior high school group was found to be 2.60, and for the junior high school group this ratio was found to be 5.11.

6. Statistically significant differences were found to exist between the school subjects preferred by mentally superior senior high school pupils and those preferred by mentally inferior senior high school pupils. Mathematics was given as the most preferred subject by 31.8 per cent of the superior boys, but was given as the

best liked subject by only 8.0 per cent of the inferior boys. Shop was the best liked subject of the mentally inferior boys, and home economics was the preferred subject of the mentally inferior girls. English was given as the most preferred subject by the superior senior high school girls. At the junior high school level the difference in subject preferences of the superior and inferior groups was much less marked than at the senior high school level.

7.   Gifted pupils at both the junior and senior high school levels take part in school activities in greater numbers than do ungifted pupils. The difference in this respect is statistically significant.

8.   Statistically significant qualitative differences were found to exist between the superior and inferior groups with respect to the types of school activities in which they engage. Whereas large numbers of superior pupils at both the junior and senior high school levels are found to be school officers and leaders, practically none of the inferior pupils are found in these categories. Pupils in the mentally inferior groups, however, take part in sports and athletics much more frequently than do pupils of superior mentality.

9.   Gifted junior and senior high school pupils more frequently have hobbies than do the ungifted pupils. The difference is statistically reliable.

10.   Differences were found to exist in the types of hobbies enjoyed by mentally superior and inferior groups. The gifted subjects frequently listed reading, building models, photography, and writing as hobbies, but not so with the ungifted subjects. The ungifted group listed as hobbies sewing, knitting, cooking, and collecting more frequently than did the gifted group. The chi-square test showed that qualitative differences obtained between the hobbies enjoyed by the gifted and the ungifted were not due to a chance selection, but were statistically significant.

11.   At both the junior and senior high school levels, superior boys read more books on biography, history, science, and travel than did mentally inferior boys. The difference in percentage divided by the standard error of the difference was 2.43 for the

senior high school group, and 1.56 for the junior high school group.

12.   Very significant differences were found between the reading interests of mentally superior and inferior pupils when the magazines they enjoy were analyzed. Mentally inferior pupils of both junior and senior high school age listed wild west, detective, mystery, movie, and pulp magazines far more frequently than did the mentally superior pupils. This was true for both boys and girls. Mentally superior pupils tend to read more expensive magazines than do mentally inferior pupils. This difference is also statistically reliable.

13.   On the knowledge of world affairs test, the gifted pupils far exceeded the ungifted. The difference divided by the standard error of the difference for the senior high school group was 20.27, and this same ratio for the junior high school was 18.00. Gifted junior high school pupils made a higher average score on the test than did the mentally retarded senior high school pupils. When the occupations of the fathers of mentally superior and inferior sophomore boys were held constant while the subjects' scores on this test were analyzed, a statistically significant difference was still found to exist in favor of the mentally superior group.

14.   Practically all the junior high school pupils plan to go to senior high school regardless of their mental ability. The per cents are 97.8 for the superior group, and 93.3 for the mentally inferior group.

15.   Practically every pupil in both the gifted and ungifted senior high school groups plans to graduate from high school. The percentages planning to do so are 99.6 for the gifted group, and 96.1 for the ungifted group.

16.   At the junior high school level, 56.7 per cent of the gifted pupils plan for a college education, while 37.3 per cent of the ungifted likewise state their intentions of entering college. The tetrachoric r between intelligence and tendency to plan for a college education at the junior high school level was found to be .16 $\pm$ .025.

17. For the senior high school group, 59.9 per cent of the gifted pupils plan to go to college as compared to 23.0 per cent of the ungifted pupils who plan to do so. The tetrachoric r between intelligence and tendency to plan for a college education at the senior high school level was found to be .31 ± .024.

18. When the intelligence of the senior high school pupils was held constant, it was found that pupils whose parents were well educated plan to go to college in greater numbers than those pupils whose parents were not well educated. Using the chi-square technique, the difference was found to be statistically significant.

19. Likewise, it was found that when the intelligence of the senior high school subjects was held constant, the occupation of the fathers proved to be a factor in determining which children plan to go to college. Gifted pupils whose fathers rate in the higher occupational levels plan to go to college more frequently than do gifted pupils whose fathers follow lowly occupations. Likewise, mentally retarded senior high school pupils whose fathers are classified in the higher occupations plan to enter college and university more frequently than do mentally retarded children whose fathers rate in the lower occupational categories. The differences in this respect were found to be statistically reliable.

20. No marked differences were found to exist between the courses planned for college by the gifted and the ungifted senior high school pupils.

21. When the occupational choices of the subjects were rated by the Brussell-Barr Scale, it was found that the gifted subjects at both the junior and senior high school levels more frequently planned careers in the higher occupations and professions than did the ungifted subjects. The differences between the gifted and the ungifted in this respect were found to be statistically reliable for all the groups, with the exception of the junior high school girls.

22. The tetrachoric r between intelligence and the tendency for junior high school boys to plan to enter the professions and high executive positions was found to be .27 ± .042. The tetra-

choric r between intelligence and the tendency of senior high school boys to plan to enter the professions and executive positions was found to be .35 $\pm$ .037.

23. Mentally superior senior high school boys whose fathers are engaged in the higher occupations tend to select occupations on a somewhat higher level than do mentally superior boys whose fathers follow lowly occupations. Using the chi-square technique, this difference was found to be statistically significant. This tendency, however, was not as marked for the mentally inferior group of senior high school boys.

The educational implications of the results of this investigation are particularly significant with respect to the differences found between the interests and ambitions of the mentally superior groups and the mentally inferior ones.

For example, the fact that pupils in the lowest 15 per cent of intelligence show very little interest in high school mathematics but express marked preferences for shop and home economics, suggests the impracticality of forcing them to take the traditional secondary school course in mathematics. Many high schools in the United States still require all pupils to take algebra and geometry if they wish to graduate.[1] It is questionable whether pupils with very limited mental ability profit at all from pursuing such courses.[2] A thorough adaptation of the secondary school curriculum to the needs of society and to the needs and abilities of the heterogeneous mass of pupils now attending these schools, is very necessary if the American High School is to survive.[3]

Education should consider it a part of its responsibility to stimulate in pupils of low mentality greater interest in school activi-

---

[1] Edwin S. Lide, *Instruction in Mathematics.* Bulletin 1932, No. 17, National Survey of Secondary Education, Monograph No. 23, p. 45. 1933.

A. K. Loomis, Edwin S. Lide, and B. Lamar Johnson, *The Program of Studies.* Bulletin 1932, No. 17, National Survey of Secondary Education, Monograph No. 19, pp. 149-152. 1933.

[2] M. V. Cobb, "Limits Set to Educational Achievement by Limited Intelligence," *Journal of Educational Psychology,* Vol. 13, pp. 449-464, and pp. 546-555. 1922.

[3] Phillip W. L. Cox, "Must the High School Survive?" *The Educational Forum,* Vol. 2, November, 1937, pp. 25-39.

ties, hobbies, and worth-while reading. It can do this by providing greater opportunities for these individuals to engage in such activities during school hours. Although the gifted pupils more frequently engage in these activities than the ungifted, a large number of them also need guidance in this respect.

Every effort should be made by the schools to develop in pupils of limited mental ability greater interest in national and world affairs. The difference between the knowledge of current events possessed by the mentally superior and mentally inferior pupils is tremendous. If democracy is to succeed in this country, all individuals must possess adequate knowledge of what is happening in the nation and the world.

The very low correlations found in this study between intelligence and the tendency of secondary school pupils to plan to enter college and eventually the professions, indicate the failure of education to provide proper guidance for its students. Education should strive to aid each individual to make satisfactory adjustments to the realities of life. "Only a relatively few should proceed through the long and somewhat tedious process of book learning that leads to the professions. The others should receive a training which not only equips them for work in certain vocations but prepares them for life as well-rounded, intelligent, and useful citizens in a democratic society." [4] To the extent that pupils hold inappropriate ambitions, to that extent has education failed to bring about the satisfactory adjustment of its pupils to the facts of life.

Data of the present investigation, however, show clearly that there is a strong relationship between the economic status of the home and the educational and vocational ambitions of pupils. No doubt many of the most superior pupils who do not plan to pursue a college education would do so if they were financially able. Society should be responsible for seeing that these individuals are not denied the opportunity of securing a higher education. How this can be done has been well stated by President Conant. He says,

[4] James Bryant Conant, "The Future of Our Higher Education," *Harpers Magazine*, Vol. 176, May, 1938, p. 564.

"There is, therefore, only one way to provide a university education for the promising youths who are now debarred by economic and geographic factors: by a generous subsidy—by large scholarships, or by providing opportunity for earning a sizeable amount of money." [5] Such a provision would make it possible for the guidance service of schools to function more effectively, and thus aid education to bring about satisfactory educational and vocational adjustments on the part of its pupils.

The results of this study show in a striking manner that secondary school pupils of superior mental ability differ significantly in many respects from their classmates who do poorly on intelligence tests. In certain of these respects, education should endeavor to reduce the differences which exist. For example, all pupils should take part in school activities, and read worth-while literature. In other respects, education should probably strive to increase the differences. This would be true in the case of the ambitions held by the superior and inferior groups.

By taking into account such facts as have been brought forth in the present investigation, secondary schools can better minister to the needs of their pupils and at the same time perform a worth-while service to society.

[5] Conant, *op. cit.*, p. 566.

BIBLIOGRAPHY

ALMACK, JOHN C. AND ALMACK, JAMES L. "Gifted Children in the High School." *School and Society*, Vol. 14, pp. 227-228, September, 1921.

BOOK, W. F. *The Intelligence of High School Seniors*. Macmillan Company, New York, 1922.

BROWN, WILLIAM. *The Essentials of Mental Measurement*. Cambridge University Press, London, 1911.

BRUSSELL, E. S. *A Study of the Composition of Juries of the District Court*. Thesis, University of Minnesota Library, Minneapolis, 1930.

BURKS, B. S., JENSEN, D. W., AND TERMAN, L. M. *The Promise of Youth Follow-up Studies of a Thousand Gifted Children*. Genetic Studies of Genius, Vol. 3. Stanford University Press, Stanford University, California, 1930.

CATTELL, J. McKEEN. "The Distribution of American Men of Science in 1932." *American Men of Science*, Fifth Edition, pp. 1265-1266. Science Press, New York, 1933.

COBB, M. V. "Limits Set to Educational Achievement by Limited Intelligence." *Journal of Educational Psychology*, Vol. 13, pp. 449-464, and pp. 546-555, November and December, 1922.

COLLMANN, R. D. *The Psychogalvanic Reactions of Exceptional and Normal School Children*. Contributions to Education, No. 469. Bureau of Publications, Teachers College, Columbia University, 1931.

CONANT, JAMES BRYANT. "The Future of Our Higher Education." *Harpers Magazine*, Vol. 176, pp. 561-570, May, 1938.

COX, PHILLIP W. L. "Must the High School Survive?" *The Educational Forum*, Vol. 2, pp. 25-39, November, 1937.

COY, GENEVIEVE. *The Interests, Abilities, and Achievements of a Special Class for Gifted Children*, Contributions to Education No. 131. Bureau of Publications, Teachers College, Columbia University, 1923.

DEICH, C. AND JONES, E. E. *A Study of Distinguished High School Pupils in Iowa*. United States Office of Education, Bulletin No. 46, Washington, 1923.

FISHER, R. A. *Statistical Methods for Research Workers*. Sixth Edition, pp. 81-119. Oliver and Boyd, London, 1936.

GARRETT, H. E. *Statistics in Psychology and Education*, Second Edition. Longmans, Green and Company, New York, 1937.

GALTON, FRANCIS. *Hereditary Genius*. Macmillan and Company, London, 1869.

GERBERICH, J. R. *A Personnel Study of 10,000 Iowa High School Seniors*. University of Iowa Studies in Education, Vol. 5, No. 3. Published by the University, Iowa City, Iowa, 1930.

HEDGE, J. W. AND HUTSON, PERCIVAL W. "A Technique for Evaluating Guidance Activities." *School Review*, Vol. 39, pp. 508-519, September, 1931.

HOLLINGWORTH, L. S. *Gifted Children: Their Nature and Nurture*. Macmillan Company, New York, 1926.

HOLLINGWORTH, L. S. "Musical Sensitivity of Children Who Test Above 135 I.Q. (Stanford-Binet)." *Journal of Educational Psychology*, Vol. 17, pp. 95-107, February, 1926.

HOLLINGWORTH, L. S. "Comparative Beauty of the Faces of Highly Intelligent

Adolescents." *Journal of Genetic Psychology,* Vol. 47, pp. 268-281, December, 1935.

JENKINS, M. D. "Socio-Psychological Study of Negro Children of Superior Intelligence." *Journal of Negro Education,* Vol. 5, pp. 175-190, April, 1936.

JOHNSON, PALMER O. AND NEYMAN, JERZY. "Tests of Certain Linear Hypotheses and Their Application to Some Educational Problems." *Statistical Research Memoirs,* Vol. 1, pp. 57-93, June, 1936.

KELLER, FRANKLIN J. AND VITELES, MORRIS S. *Vocational Guidance Throughout the World: A Comparative Study.* W. W. Norton Company, New York, 1937.

KOLOZZIEJCZYK, STANISLAW. "On an Important Class of Statistical Hypotheses." *Biometrika,* Vol. 27, pp. 161-190, March, 1935.

KOOS, LEONARD V. AND KEFAUVER, GRAYSON N. *Guidance in Secondary Schools.* Macmillan Company, New York, 1934.

LAMSON, E. E. *A Study of Young Gifted Children in Senior High School.* Contributions to Education, No. 424. Bureau of Publications, Teachers College, Columbia University, 1930.

LIDE, EDWIN S. *Instruction in Mathematics.* Bulletin 1932, No. 17, National Survey of Secondary Education, Monograph No. 23. Government Printing Office, Washington, 1933.

LOOMIS, A. K., LIDE, EDWIN S., AND JOHNSON, B. LAMAR. *The Programs of Studies.* Bulletin 1932, No. 17, National Survey of Secondary Education, Monograph No. 19. Government Printing Office, Washington, 1933.

McELWEE, E. W. "A Comparison of the Personality Traits of 300 Accelerated, Normal, and Retarded Children." *Journal of Educational Research,* Vol. 26, pp. 31-34, September, 1932.

MONAHAN, J. E. AND HOLLINGWORTH, L. S. "Neuromuscular Capacity of Children Who Test Above 135 I.Q. (Stanford-Binet)." *Journal of Educational Psychology,* Vol. 18, pp. 88-96, February, 1927.

MOORE, MARGARET WHITESIDE. *A Study of Young High School Graduates.* Contributions to Education, No. 583. Bureau of Publications, Teachers College, Columbia University, 1933.

PATERSON, DONALD G. *Research Studies in Individual Diagnosis,* Vol. 3, No. 4. University of Minnesota Employment Stabilization Research Institute, August, 1934.

PEARSON, KARL. *Tables for Statisticians and Biometricians,* Part 1, third edition. University College, London, 1930.

PETERS, C. C. AND VAN VOORHIS, W. R. *Statistical Procedures and Their Mathematical Bases.* Pennsylvania State College, State College, Pennsylvania, 1935.

PORTENIER, LILLIAN G. *Pupils of Low Mentality in High School.* Contributions to Education, No. 568. Bureau of Publications, Teachers College, Columbia University, 1933.

SCHEIDEMANN, N. V. *The Psychology of Exceptional Children.* Houghton Mifflin Company, Boston, 1931.

SNEDECOR, GEORGE W. *Calculation and Interpretation of Analysis of Variance and Covariance.* Collegiate Press, Incorporated, Ames, Iowa, 1934.

TERMAN, L. M. *The Mental and Physical Traits of a Thousand Gifted Children.* Genetic Studies of Genius, Vol. 1. Stanford University Press, Stanford University, California, 1925.

United States Office of Education Bulletin, No. 2, Chapter 1 of the Biennial Survey of Education in the United States, Washington, 1933.

United States Office of Education Bulletin, No. 2, Chapter 2 of the Biennial Survey of Education in the United States, Washington, 1935.

VAN DENBURG, JOSEPH K. *Causes of the Elimination of Students in Public Secondary Schools of New York City.* Contributions to Education, No. 47. Bureau of Publications, Teachers College, Columbia University, 1911.

VISHER, STEPHEN S. "The Comparative Rank of American States." *American Journal of Sociology,* Vol. 36, pp. 735-757, March, 1931.

WITTY, PAUL A. *A Study of One Hundred Gifted Children.* Bureau of School Service and Research, University of Kansas, Lawrence, Kansas, 1930.

YATES, DOROTHY H. *A Study of Some High School Seniors of Superior Intelligence.* Journal of Educational Research Monographs, No. 2. Public School Publishing Company, Bloomington, 1922.

YERKES, R. M. (Editor). *Psychological Examining in the United States Army.* Memoirs of the National Academy of Sciences, Vol. 15. Government Printing Office, Washington, 1921.

APPENDICES

APPENDIX A

LIST OF OCCUPATIONS WHICH MENTALLY SUPERIOR AND INFERIOR
PUPILS PLAN TO FOLLOW AS LIFE CAREERS

Occupation	SENIOR HIGH SCHOOL				JUNIOR HIGH SCHOOL			
	Boys		Girls		Boys		Girls	
	Superior N=96	Inferior N=75	Superior N=80	Inferior N=80	Superior N=80	Inferior N=81	Superior N=82	Inferior N=67
Archeologist............					1			
Architect..............	2	1	1		1	1		
Astronomer............					1			
Chemist...............	2	1			1	2	1	
Diplomatic, state, and naval officials.........	3				1		1	
Engineer (civil, electrical, chemical, mechanical, mining, etc.).........	23	6			18	4		
Forestry expert.........	2	2			3	1		
Lawyer................	6	1		1	4		1	
Physician or surgeon....	8	3			2	2	2	1
Psychiatrist...........				1				
Scientist..............	1		2				1	
Accountant............	3						1	1
Business administrator ..	1		1					
Captain of a ship.......	1							
Great singer...........								1
High school teacher.....	6	3	7	1	1	2	6	1
Journalist.............	2		9		2	1	4	
Large land holder.......						1		
Missionary............							1	
Pharmacist............	1		2					
Veterinarian...........		1						
Writer................			1		1		1	
Actress...............			1				1	
Air stewardess.........			2	1			3	
Automobile dealer......					1			
Aviator...............	6	5			17	8	3	3
Bookkeeper...........	5		1				4	3
Business owner........	3	2			3	1		
Buyer for a store.......								1
Chiropractor..........					1			

APPENDIX A (*continued*)

Occupation	SENIOR HIGH SCHOOL				JUNIOR HIGH SCHOOL			
	Boys		Girls		Boys		Girls	
	Supe-rior N=96	In-ferior N=75	Supe-rior N=80	In-ferior N=80	Supe-rior N=80	In-ferior N=81	Supe-rior N=82	In-ferior N=67
Clerk in a bank.........			1					
Commercial artist.......			2	3	1	2	1	1
Costume designer.......	1			1			4	1
Detective..............		2			1	1		
Dietician..............				1			1	1
Draftsman.............		1			1			
Dramatist.............				2				
Food inspector.........		1						
Furniture business......		1						
Grade school teacher....		1	7	6		1	8	3
Home economics expert..				1				
Interior decorator.......				2			1	
Laboratory technician...			1				1	
Librarian..............			1					1
Mail clerk on train......						1		
Mortician.............		1						
Music teacher.........		1					2	
Musician..............	2	1	3	2			8	8
Nurse................			9	12			3	18
Photographer..........		1						
Printer...............		1						
Radio operator.........	2	2			1			
Railroad engineer.......		1			1			
Showman..............						1		
Social worker..........				1				
Stenographer, secretary..		2	22	25			19	7
Telegraph operator......						1		
Traveling salesman......	1							
Y.M.C.A. secretary.....	1							
Carpenter.............	1	2				3		
Diesel engineer.........	3	4			1	2		
Dressmaker...........				1			1	
Electrician............		5				3		
Farming..............					3	5		
Filing clerk...........	1	1						3
Florist...............			1				2	
Forest ranger..........		3				1		
House painter.........		1			1			
Machinist.............	1	1			1			
Meat business.........	1							

APPENDIX A (*continued*)

Occupation	Senior High School				Junior High School			
	Boys		Girls		Boys		Girls	
	Superior N=96	Inferior N=75	Superior N=80	Inferior N=80	Superior N=80	Inferior N=81	Superior N=82	Inferior N=67
Mechanic	3	7			2	10		
Professional athlete	1				1	1		
Sales clerk		3	4	4		4	1	4
Stationary engineer		2				3		
Tailor				1				
Typist				1				2
Undertaker						1		
Watchmaker		1						
Beauty shop operator			1	9				4
Butcher		1						
Concrete mixer						1		
Fishing					1	1		
Hospital attendant				1				
Letter carrier					1	1		
Milliner's helper				1				
Millworker		1			1	2		
Railroad brakeman						1		
Railroad switchman					1			
Sailor	2				2	6		
Soldier		1						
Theater usher				1				1
Trapper	1							
Truck driver		1				1		
Tugboat worker					1	1		
Waitress								2
City scavenger						1		
Common laborer		1				3		
Logger		1						
Longshoreman						1		

APPENDIX B

STATES AND FOREIGN COUNTRIES IN WHICH THE PARENTS OF THE MENTALLY SUPERIOR AND INFERIOR CHILDREN WERE BORN

Place	Senior High Group Superior N=412	Inferior N=404	Junior High Group Superior N=384	Inferior N=324	Total Superior N=796	Inferior N=728
North Atlantic States:						
Maine	3	2	1	1	4	3
New Hampshire		1		2		3
Vermont			1		1	
Massachusetts	4	1	2	1	6	2
Connecticut		1	1		1	1
New York	7	3	5	3	12	6
New Jersey	1				1	
Pennsylvania	15	7	5	3	20	10
South Atlantic States:						
Maryland		2		1		3
Virginia	1	2		2	1	4
West Virginia	1	2	1		2	2
North Carolina		3	3	4	3	7
South Carolina			1		1	
Georgia	2	1	1		3	1
Florida			1	1	1	1
South Central States:						
Kentucky	3	6	1	7	4	13
Tennessee	1	5			1	5
Mississippi	1			1	1	1
Louisiana			1		1	
Texas	3	3	3	4	6	7
Oklahoma	5	2	3	4	8	6
Arkansas	3	2	1	6	4	8
North Central States:						
Minnesota	34	35	40	39	74	74
Wisconsin	30	30	28	13	58	43
Michigan	22	28	23	7	45	35
Nebraska	15	5	12	5	27	10
Kansas	13	12	10	6	23	18
Indiana	14	2	8	4	22	6
Illinois	14	10	14	7	28	17
Iowa	9	20	9	11	18	31
Ohio	6	2	5	4	11	6
North Dakota	8	14	16	13	24	27

APPENDIX B (*continued*)

Place	SENIOR HIGH GROUP		JUNIOR HIGH GROUP		TOTAL	
	Superior $N=412$	Inferior $N=404$	Superior $N=384$	Inferior $N=324$	Superior $N=796$	Inferior $N=728$
South Dakota	5	6	2	4	7	10
Missouri	19	13	11	10	30	23
Western States:						
Washington	52	38	59	31	111	69
Oregon	7	3	8	1	15	4
California	6		4	6	10	6
Utah	5	1	4		9	1
Colorado	1	2	8	1	9	3
Wyoming	1		3	2	4	2
Montana	2	9	4	11	6	20
Idaho	3	4	6	6	9	10
Foreign Countries:						
Norway	31	41	15	33	46	74
Sweden	10	21	12	10	22	31
Canada	10	27	15	14	25	41
Italy	4	5		6	4	11
Finland	6	1	1		7	1
England	11	7	8	4	19	11
Holland	6	5	2	4	8	9
Ireland	2	3	1	4	3	7
Scotland	3	3	5	5	8	8
Germany	4	7	5	2	9	9
Denmark	2	1	2	2	4	3
Russia	2		2	2	4	2
Jugoslavia	2		2		4	
Czechoslovakia	1		2	2	3	2
France	1			1	1	1
Mexico	1				1	
Rumania		1				1
Japan		2	2		2	2
China		2				2
Poland		1		4		5
Belgium			2	3	2	3
Greece			1	5	1	5
Austria			2	2	2	2

APPENDIX C

SENIOR HIGH SCHOOL

Name................................Date................Class...................
Birthdate..................Nationality...............Birthplace.................
Major subject................Minor subject...........................
Do you plan to finish high school?.................... If not, what do you plan to do?...................
Do you expect to enter college or university when you finish high school?.............
Which college?.................... What course will you take?....................
Do you plan to get a steady job when you graduate from high school?...............
What kind of a job?....................
Give other plans you may have....................
What occupation do you expect to follow as a life's work?....................
What would be your second choice of an occupation?....................
Of all the subjects you have taken, name the one you like best...................
Name the subject you like second best....................
Name the two subjects you like least (1)....................(2)....................
What is the present occupation of your father?....................
What other occupations has your father followed?....................
Occupation of your grandfather on your father's side....................
Occupation of your grandfather on your mother's side....................
Father's birthplace....................Mother's birthplace....................

Check how much education your parents have had:		Father	Mother
	Less than 8th grade		
(Remember that when your	8th grade graduate		
parents were young there	Some high school work		
were very few high schools.)	High school graduate		
	Some college work		
	College graduate		

How many brothers and sisters have you?....................
In what school activities have you participated?....................
Do you have any hobbies?....................What are they?....................
Name two books you have enjoyed reading (1)....................(2)....................
Name two magazines you enjoy reading (1)....................(2)....................

QUESTIONNAIRE

JUNIOR HIGH SCHOOL

Name....................................Date....................Class....................
Birthdate..................Nationality...............Birthplace....................
When you finish junior high school, do you plan to enter senior high school?.............
If not, what are your plans?....................
What course will you take at high school?....................
When you finish high school, do you expect to go to college or university?.............
Which college?....................What course will you take?....................

Do you plan to get a steady job when you graduate from high school?..................
What kind of a job?...
Give other plans you may have...
What occupation do you expect to follow as a life's work?.................................
What would be your second choice of an occupation?.................................:..............
Of all the subjects you have taken, name the one you like best.........................
Name the subject you like second best...
Name the two subjects you like least (1)...........................(2)...........................
What is the present occupation of your father?...
What other occupations has your father followed?...
Occupation of your grandfather on your father's side..................................·....................
Occupation of your grandfather on your mother's side...
Father's birthplace.................................Mother's birthplace.................................

Check how much education your parents have had:

		Father	Mother
	Less than 8th grade	....	....
(Remember that when your	8th grade graduate	....	....
parents were young there	Some high school work	....	....
were not as many schools as	High school graduate	....	....
there are today.)	Some college work	....	....
	College graduate	....	....

How many brothers and sisters have you? ....
In what school activities have you participated? ....
Do you have any hobbies?...........................What are they?.................................
Name two books you have enjoyed reading (1)...........................(2)...........................
Name two magazines you enjoy reading (1)...........................(2)...........................

APPENDIX D

BRUSSELL–BARR SCALE OF OCCUPATIONAL INTELLIGENCE*

I. HIGH PROFESSIONAL AND EXECUTIVE OCCUPATIONS
(Requiring very superior intelligence)

Sigma Score	Occupation	Description
70.65	Research leader	Like Binet, Pasteur, etc.
70.65	Writer, great	Van Dyke, etc.
70.65	Surgeon, great	Mayo brothers, etc.
70.65	Inventive genius	Edison type
70.65	Lawyer	Eminent
70.24	Engineer, consulting	In charge of a corps of engineers
69.84	Merchant, great	Owns and operates a million dollar business
69.35	Editor	Large city paper, or head of national magazine
68.95	Engineer, civil	Requires 4–5 years college training. In charge of plans and construction of bridges, roads, etc.
68.63	President	College
68.63	Professor, University	Has A.M. or Ph.D., writes, teaches, and does reasearch
68.63	Architect	Training equal to college graduate
68.23	Judge	Municipal, district, federal
67.82	Scientist, applied	Bacteriologist, psychologist, sociologist, etc.
67.42	Physician or surgeon	Average, 6–8 years post-high school training
67.26	Engineer, mining	Thorough knowledge of mining and extraction of metals
67.02	Officials, mfg.	Heads of large companies
66.61	Banker	Executive head of fairly large bank
66.61	Statistician	Engaged in original research in statistics, college training in mathematics necessary
66.21	Chemist, industrial	Thorough knowledge of chemistry of manufacturing processes
65.97	Engineer, mechanical	Designs and constructs machines and machine tools
65.97	Official or inspector	State, federal, cabinet officer, diplomat, etc.
65.73	Engineer, technical	Thorough knowledge of processes of industry

II. LOWER PROFESSIONAL AND LARGE BUSINESS OCCUPATIONS
(Requiring superior intelligence)

65.56	Musician, great	Voice or instrumental (Paderewski)

* See Brussell reference listed on page 12.

Sigma Score	Occupation	Description
65.16	Officials and superintendents	Railroad
65.00	Accountant or auditor	Private or public, 4 years of college
64.27	Educational administrator	Superintendent or principal of schools
64.27	Dentist, great	In city
64.27	Artist	High class painter of portraits, etc.
63.39	Stockbroker	Head or manager of a company; has detailed knowledge of stocks and bonds
62.98	Teacher, college	Has A.B. or A.M.; not the most progressive
62.58	Preacher, average	College graduate
62.58	Social worker	Supervisor or head of department; college training required
62.58	Music composer	
62.58	Salesman, technical	College trained
61.77	Lawyer	Average in moderate size city; income $1000–$5000
61.37	Teacher, high school	College graduate
61.37	Secretary	Private secretary to high government official, business, or professional man
60.97	Writer	Magazine or books, light fiction, or nonfiction
60.79	Banker, bank officials	Small town or small bank
60.56	Pharmacist	Graduate of college
60.56	Advertisement writer	Plans and writes copy
60.56	Land owner and operator	Very large farm or ranch
60.16	Osteopath	Training equal to college graduate
59.95	Manager or superintendent	Average size factory
59.95	Veterinary doctor	Special training, some college work
59.35	Reporter	On newspaper; assigned articles or feature stories
59.19	Editor	Small paper; considerable job work
58.79	Teacher, art	In high school; 3–4 years special training

III. TECHNICAL, CLERICAL, AND SUPERVISORY OCCUPATIONS
(Requiring high average intelligence)

Sigma Score	Occupation	Description
58.55	Builder or contractor	In charge of construction
58.55	Actor	Successful in drama or musical productions
58.31	Artist	Cartoonist or illustrator for papers or magazines
57.90	Dentist	Small town
57.74	Y.M.C.A. officials	Secretary, etc.
57.34	Manufacturer	Employs from 10–50 men
57.34	Compiler	Of census, bibliographies, etc.
56.94	Aviator	Flyer; involves technical knowledge of aeronautics

Sigma Score	Occupation	Description
56.94	Appraiser	Estimates values for insurance companies, etc.
55.81	Draftsman	Mechanical
55.73	Teacher, grammar school	Normal graduate and expects to make profession of teaching
55.73	Stock and bond salesman	Employee of company
55.32	Druggist	Retail dealer
55.32	Mechanic, master	Thorough knowledge of his field of mechanics
55.32	Showman	Manager of theatrical productions; drama, movies
55.32	Lumberman	Owner or manager of lumber camps or company
54.92	Librarian	In small institution or public library
54.92	Hotel keeper	Owns or manages average hotel
54.92	Commercial broker and commission man	Wholesaler dealer in fruits, grains, livestock, etc.
54.52	Teacher, primary grades	No college training; two years special training
54.52	Bookkeeper	Training equivalent to high school or business college
54.52	Social worker	Routine work; writing case histories, etc.; may be gained by practical experience
54.52	Surveyor	Transit man, city or county
54.52	Train dispatcher	Must be mentally alert
54.11	Statistician	Clerical work; manipulation of formulae under supervision
54.11	Foreman	Large factory
54.11	Teacher, music	Not in high school; 2–4 years special training; not a college graduate
54.11	Optician	Retail dealer
54.11	Detective	Traces clues; employee of detective bureau
54.11	Caterer	Owner or in charge of directing the catering service
53.71	Teacher, athletics or dancing	Special training
53.71	Wholesale dealer	Fairly small; includes exporter and importer
53.71	Jeweler	Retail dealer
53.71	Automobile dealer	Owner or manager of average size shop or business
53.63	Official or inspector	City or county
53.31	Radio announcer	
53.31	Salesman, travelling	Wholesale; orders taken from stores for clothing, etc.
53.31	Stenographer	Writes shorthand and uses typewriter

Sigma Score	Occupation	Description
52.90	Real estate agent	Sells or rents property on commission basis
52.90	Salesman, travelling	Retail; sells drugs, groceries, dry-goods, etc.
52.82	Nurseryman	Owner or manager
52.50	Insurance agent	Sells policies for a company
52.50	Costumer	Retail dealer; for men or women
52.50	Telegraph operator	Special training and skill
52.50	Gardener	Truck farming; owns and operates small plots
52.50	Conductor	On railroad passenger train
52.42	Musician	Successful player or singer in a good company
52.10	Chiropractor	Special training required—about 1 year; not a college graduate
52.10	Hardware dealer	Retail
52.10	Foreman	Small factory or shop
51.94	Foreman	In transportation
51.69	Haberdasher	Retail dealer
51.69	Shipping clerk	In wholesale company; in charge of receiving or sending goods
51.29	Radio operator	In broadcasting station
51.29	Agent, express or freight	In charge of department
51.29	Nurse and masseur	Graduate from accredited hospital
50.89	Photographer	A few months training, and experience required
50.89	Undertaker	Funeral director
50.89	Printer	Of small shop; job work
50.89	Furrier	Retail dealer
50.89	Mail clerk	Railroad
50.65	Keeper	Of charitable institution
50.48	Floorwalker and foreman	In stores; in charge of department; may direct sales clerks
50.48	Chef	Employed in first-class hotels
50.48	Gardener	Landscape
50.08	Garage keeper	Retail dealer
50.08	Waiter, head	In hotel or restaurant; in charge of dining room waiters

IV. SKILLED TRADESMEN AND LOW GRADE CLERICAL WORKERS
(Requiring average intelligence)

Sigma Score	Occupation	Description
50.00	Electrotyper	Prepares wood cuts
49.84	Lithographer	Makes prints from designs which he puts on stones
49.84	Sheriff	County
49.68	Tailor	Retail dealer
49.68	Aeroplane mechanic	Technical knowledge as well as mechanical skill
49.68	Station agent	In small town; acts as baggage man, freight agent, operator, etc.

Sigma Score	Occupation	Description
49.44	Pattern maker	Wood
49.44	Pattern maker	Metal
49.27	Auctioneer	General
49.27	Milliner	Owner; makes hats in small establishment; may have a few helpers
49.27	Grocer	Retail dealer
49.27	Musician	In orchestra or band
49.27	Linotype operator	
49.27	Notary public	
49.27	Buyer of livestock	Retail dealer
49.03	Farmer	Owner or manager of moderate sized tract of land
48.87	Jeweler	Maker of watches in factory
48.87	Piano or organ tuner	Requires knowledge of the construction of musical instruments
48.47	Florist	Retail dealer
48.47	Policeman	Sergeant or chief
48.47	Chiropodist	Requiring only special training; not a medical course
48.23	Restaurant keeper	Small cafe or restaurant
48.15	Dressmaker	At home or in small shop; may employ a few helpers
48.06	Athlete	Professional; depends upon this for his income
48.06	Express clerk	In charge of desk, receiving or sending
47.74	Typesetter	In printing shop or for newspaper, etc.
47.66	Dairyman	Retail dealer
47.66	Book binder	Sets up and binds books of all sorts
47.42	Engineer, stationary	In coal mines, brakeman, etc.; requires mainly specialized training as operative
47.26	Repairman, mechanical	In shop or factory; keeps machines in condition
46.85	Inspector, sampler, etc.	In factory, railroad, etc.
46.85	Upholsterer	Renovator of furniture, etc.; small shop
46.45	Potter	Makes jugs, jars, crockery, earthen ware, etc.
46.45	Mechanic, average	Auto mechanic
46.45	Telephone operator	Special training
46.45	Butcher	Retail dealer
46.05	Collector	Employed to collect debts, etc.
46.05	Electric repairman	Repairs electric utensils, devices, and machines
46.05	Baker	Retail dealer
46.05	Chauffeur	Including taxicab drivers; some knowledge of auto mechanics
45.65	Ticket agent	Employed in depots, ticket offices, etc.

Sigma Score	Occupation	Description
45.65	Forest ranger	Looks for forest fires, etc.
45.65	Barber	Owner of shop
45.65	Tinsmith	Makes vessels, utensils, from plated sheet metal
45.56	Undertaker	Embalmer; 6 months to 1 year of special training
45.56	Stone mason	
45.24	Typist	No shorthand, types from copy
45.24	Repairman, general	Repairs broken articles; uses wood working tools
45.16	Actor	Vaudeville or variety; singing, dancing, acrobatics, etc.
45.16	Pseudo-scientist	Fortune teller, astrologist, spiritualist, healer, etc.
44.84	Cashier	Makes change; retail stores, etc.
44.84	Clerk, stock	Checks stocks
44.84	Plumber	Average trained plumber (employee)
44.44	Moving picture operator	Operates machine which projects pictures
44.44	Fruitman	Retail dealer
44.44	Telegraph and telephone lineman	Installs and repairs system
44.44	Mechanic, average	In foundry
44.44	Carpenter	Knows wood working tools; can follow directions in various processes of wood construction
44.44	Plasterer	Knowledge of materials used is necessary
44.03	Agent and canvasser	House to house canvassing and demonstrating
44.03	Apiarist	Keeper of bees
44.03	Tailor	Not owner, works in tailor shop
43.87	Harness maker	Leather work
43.63	Clerk, sales	Retail selling from counter; grocery, department store, etc.
43.63	Painter	Paints houses, etc.
43.23	Graphotype operator	
43.23	Fishmonger	Retail dealer
43.23	Tire repairman	In general auto repair shop; knowledge of vulcanizing
43.06	Conductor	Street car
42.82	Filing clerk	Little technical knowledge; quite routine

V. SEMI-SKILLED OCCUPATIONS
(Requiring low average or slightly below average intelligence)

Sigma Score	Occupation	Description
42.42	Letter carrier	
42.02	Structural steel-worker	Heavy work, demanding some skill

Sigma Score	Occupation	Description
42.02	News dealer	Retail dealer
41.61	Motorman	Street railway
41.37	Painter	Or glazier, varnisher; in factory
41.21	Policeman	Average patrolman
41.08	Farm tenant	On small tract of land
41.08	Cooper	In factory
40.97	Fire fighter, city	Handles the ordinary fire fighting apparatus
40.81	Fireman, railroad	On freight or passenger trains
40.00	Hairdresser, manicurist	Employed in shops
39.68	Metal finisher	Polishes and lacquers metal fixtures, etc.
39.60	Brakeman	On freight or passenger trains
39.19	Cobbler and shoemaker	Repairer in shoe shop
39.19	Cook	In restaurant or small shop
38.79	Smelter worker	Castings, etc.
38.79	Bricklayer	Laborer
38.79	Baker	Not owner; employee engaged in the making of baked goods
38.39	Butcher	Not shop owner; able to make cuts properly
38.39	Pop corn stand or confectionary keeper	Retail dealer
38.39	Deliveryman	Delivers groceries, etc., with auto
38.39	Dressmakers helper	Finishing work, routine
37.98	Ship rigger	Installing cordage system on sailing vessel; working under supervision
37.98	Factory operative	Operates machines; semi-skilled
37.58	Barber	Not owner; has charge of chair
37.58	Messenger boy	In office or store
37.58	Milliner's helper	Employee of milliner, under supervision
37.18	Switchman and flagman	Tending switch in railroad yard
37.18	Waiter	In small restaurant or café
36.77	Janitor or sexton	
36.77	Bar tender	
36.37	Laborer	In factory; such as packers, wrappers, counters, etc.
36.37	Laundry worker	Various kinds of work in laundry; practically unskilled
36.37	Teamster	Drayman, expressman
36.29	Porter	Personal service on train, etc.
36.29	Maid servant	Personal or domestic work
35.97	Waterworks man	A variety of jobs, all practically unskilled
35.89	Worker	In factory, such as metal, leather, textile; practically no skill
35.56	Odd job man	
34.76	Hospital attendant	Carries meal trays, etc.
34.76	Baggage man	Or drayman; transports baggage under supervision

Sigma Score	Occupation	Description
34.76	Miner	Digger and shoveler
34.76	Saw mill worker	Heavy work; little skill required
34.35	Dairy hand	Milking, care of stock, under supervision
34.35	Fisherman	Employee or engaged in the work of catching fish

VI. Unskilled Occupations
(Requiring inferior intelligence only)

Sigma Score	Occupation	Description
33.95	Hostler	Cares for horses in livery; feeds; cleans stables
33.95	Junkman	Collector of junk
33.95	Guard, watchman, or doorkeeper	Routine work
33.55	Lumberman	Laborer
33.31	Elevator tender	Routine work, requiring little knowledge or training
31.94	Longshoreman	Loads and unloads cargoes
30.73	Garbage collector	
30.73	Hobo	Vagrant
30.32	Section hand, railroad	Replaces ties, etc., under supervision
30.32	Circus roustabout	Does heavy work about the circus
30.32	Day laborer	On street, in shop or factory as a roustabout
30.32	Farm laborer	Unskilled and usually inefficient

VITA

Glenn Myers Blair was born at Portland, Oregon, October 2, 1908.

Academic Training:

A.B. Seattle Pacific College, Seattle, 1930;
A.M. University of Washington, Seattle, 1931;
Denny Fellow, University of Washington, 1931-32;
Teachers College Fellow, Columbia University, 1937-38;
Summer sessions, University of Washington, 1935, and Columbia University, 1936.

Experience:

Instructor in mathematics and psychological counselor, Sedro-Woolley High School, Sedro-Woolley, Washington, 1932-33;
Head, mathematics department, Bremerton High School, Bremerton, Washington, 1933-36;
Director, department of research and guidance, Everett, Washington Public Schools, 1936-37;
Visiting professor in educational measurements, University of Washington, Summer 1937;
Visiting professor in educational psychology, University of Kansas, Summer 1938;
Instructor in educational psychology, University of Illinois, 1938-

Publications and Research:

The Prediction of Freshman Success in the University of Washington. Master's Thesis, University of Washington Library, Seattle, 1931. "What About Tests in Guidance?" *Washington Education Journal,* Vol. 16, February, 1937.

DATE DUE